available at
amazon

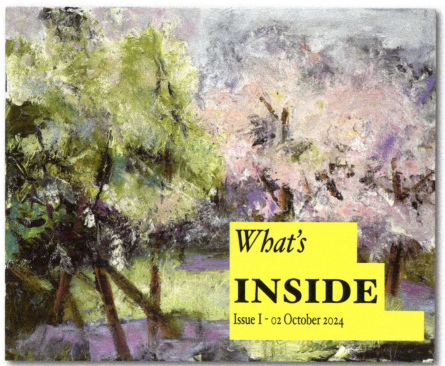

SPRING TREES, 24 X 30 by Janet H. Dilenschneider
A vibrant celebration of renewal, this painting captures the essence of spring with its lively colors and dynamic composition, inviting viewers to experience the rejuvenating energy of nature's awakening.

Cover
Painting Hope and Harmony

18 JANET HENNESSEY DILENSCHNEIDER
How Nature and Expressionism Shape Her Visionary Art issues.

Janet Hennessey Dilenschneider, an expressionist painter, draws inspiration from nature to create serene landscapes. Her work emphasizes hope and beauty, encouraging viewers to connect with art and environmental issues.

Literature

6 P.C. JAMES
From Childhood Inspirations to Beloved Series

7 S. LEE FISHER
A Tale of Resilience, Independence, and Storytelling

8 JOSEPH FAGARAZZI
Inspires with resilience and self-belief

9. ROBERT EMMERS
Turning Real-Life Adventures into Riveting Fiction

Art & Media

10 RACHAEL BLAKEY
Freezing Moments

12 JANUARIO JANO
Exploring the Intersections

14 YANA BARABASH
Discovering Beauty in Layers

16 SOFIA RUIZ
Memory and Emotion

Business

28 *Why Financial Planning Is a Great Career Option for Women P.28*

30 ENIS HULLI
Pioneering Global Success from Emerging Europe

32 CANDICE ELLIOTT
Pioneering Strategic HR Leadership

34 FREDERIK STEENSGAARD
Leading the Charge

Beauty

36 DAR BAROT
The Creative Maestro Redefining Beauty

38 ELENA
Empowering Women's Wellness Journey

40 SIMONE THOSMAS
Empowering Women's Wellness Journey

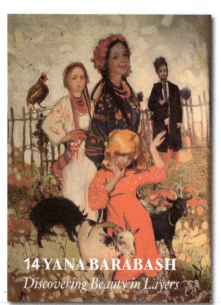

14 YANA BARABASH
Discovering Beauty in Layers

PUBLISHER: Mosaic Digest, A Subsidiary of NewYox Media Group. 200 Suite 134-146 Curtain Road, EC2A 3AR London, United Kingdom
t: +44 79 3847 8420 editor@mosaicdigest.com II http://newyox.com
EDITORIAL: Hazel Ivy, Editor-in-Chief, Arch Preston, Managing Editor, C. Rochelle, Art Editor, Delfina Reneta, Content Editor,
Reporters: Jack Wilson, Jenny Taylor, J. Evans, Amy Browm CONTRIBUTOS: Claudine D. Reyes, Esma Arslan, Adrian T.
We assume no responsibility for unsolicited manuscripts or art materials provided from our contributors.

From the Editor's Desk

Welcome to the inaugural issue of Mosaic Digest, where our slogan, *"Every Story, Every Angle,"* comes to life. We are thrilled to embark on this journey with you, exploring the vibrant tapestry of human narratives that span the globe. At Mosaic Digest, we believe every story deserves to be told and celebrated, and every angle explored. Our mission is to bring you a rich blend of stories that capture the essence of human experience, from the creative realms of art and music to the dynamic worlds of business and fashion, and from the profound insights of literature to the strategic intricacies of management.

While this is our first issue, we are not new to the world of magazine publishing. Our sister magazine, Reader's House, is set to release its 50th issue next month, proudly available in print across 190 countries and through thousands of retailers and platforms, including Amazon, Barnes & Noble, Walmart, and Waterstones. Mosaic Digest will soon join these ranks, bringing our unique perspective to readers worldwide.

We are honored to feature the renowned expressionist painter Janet Hennessey Dilenschneider on the cover of our first issue. Janet's work is a testament to the transformative power of art, drawing inspiration from nature to create serene landscapes that emphasize hope and beauty. Her latest exhibition, *"Come To The Light,"* is a beacon of peace and solace in a troubled world, inviting viewers to connect with art and environmental issues. In our exclusive interview, Janet shares her creative process, influences, and dedication to using art as a medium for social commentary. Her journey, from a chance encounter with Roy Lichtenstein to her current status as a celebrated artist, is as inspiring as her work.

In this issue, we also delve into the world of literature, featuring authors who have captivated readers with their unique voices. P.C. James takes us on a journey from childhood inspirations to a beloved series, while S. Lee Fisher shares a tale of resilience, independence, and storytelling. Joseph Fagarazzi inspires with his message of resilience and self-belief, and Robert Emmers turns real-life adventures into riveting fiction.

In the realm of art and media, we explore the works of Rachael Blakey, who captures the essence of fleeting moments, and Januario Jano, who delves into the intersections of art and culture. Yana Barabash invites us to discover beauty in layers, while Sofia Ruiz explores the depths of memory and emotion.

Our business section highlights the importance of financial planning as a career option for women, with insights from Enis Hulli, who is pioneering global success from emerging Europe, and Candice Elliott, a leader in strategic HR. Frederik Steensgaard is leading the charge in innovative business practices, and P.C. James returns to share his journey from childhood inspirations to a beloved series.

In beauty, we feature Dar Barot, the creative maestro redefining beauty, and Elena and Simone Thomas, who are empowering women's wellness journeys.

We invite you to immerse yourself in the diverse stories and perspectives that Mosaic Digest has to offer. As we embark on this exciting journey, we hope to inspire, inform, and connect with you through the power of storytelling.

Thank you for joining us on this adventure.

Hazel Ivy
Editor-in-Chief

Literature

From Childhood Inspirations to Beloved Series

P.C. James discusses his inspirations, character development, historical research, and the integration of humor and wildlife photography into his beloved cozy mystery series.

by Jack Wilson

Crafting Historical Settings with Authenticity

Acclaimed author P.C. James has carved a niche for himself in the cozy mystery genre, delighting readers with his series such as the Miss Riddell Cozy Mysteries, the One Man and His Dog Cozy Mysteries, and the Royal Duchess and Sassy Senior Sleuths cozy mysteries, co-authored with Kathryn Mykel. Residing near Toronto, Canada, James balances his passion for wildlife photography with his dedication to crafting engaging narratives, often drawing inspiration from his own experiences and memories.

James's journey into the world of cozy mysteries began during his childhood and young adulthood, when he would spend wet summer holidays at his aunts' house in Ravenscar, facing the North Sea. The inclement Northern English weather provided ample time for him to delve into the mysteries of Christie, Sayers, and Heyer. However, the defining moment came much later, when he watched Joan Hickson's portrayal of Miss Marple. This experience, combined with fond memories of his aunts and their mystery books, brought the character of Miss Riddell to life almost naturally.

In the One Man and His Dog series, James introduces Tom Ramsay, a retired inspector with a loyal border collie. Ramsay's character is inspired by the steady, serious men in James's family, who were not given to emotional outbursts. Ramsay's unorthodox approach to law enforcement, coupled with his compassion and ability to see the many sides of people, makes him a unique and relatable protagonist. James's own experience of retirement adds an authentic touch to Ramsay's character, making his stories even more compelling.

Historical settings play a significant role in James's books, particularly England in the 1950s and 1960s. Drawing from his own vivid memories of childhood and teenage years, James ensures the accuracy of these periods through meticulous research. He checks his recollections and delves into the songs and movies of the time to create a rich, immersive backdrop for his narratives.

In his new series co-authored with Kathryn Mykel, The Duchess of Snodsbury Amateur Detective Series, James explores the intriguing dynamics of an aristocratic setting. The collaboration between James and Mykel, who writes quilting craft-based cozy mysteries, brings together their unique perspectives and expertise. Set in England in the Fifties, a time when crafts were everyday skills, this series offers a delightful blend of historical accuracy and engaging storytelling.

Humor is a notable element in James's Miss Riddell Cozy Mysteries. Inspired by his admiration for Jane Austen's writing style, James skillfully balances humor with suspense and intrigue. This approach not only keeps readers engaged but also adds depth to his characters and their relationships.

James's love for wildlife photography often finds its way into his books. His experiences with nature photography have inspired scenes and characters, adding an authentic touch to his narratives. For instance, his own Galapagos cruise experience is vividly depicted in "Murder on a Galapagos Cruise," where a fellow guest's humorous reaction to seeing more iguanas is incorporated into the story. Similarly, his wildlife photography experience enriches the two books set in Australia.

P.C. James's ability to blend personal experiences, historical accuracy, and engaging storytelling has made him a beloved author in the cozy mystery genre. His unique characters, rich settings, and the delicate balance of humor and suspense continue to captivate readers, making his books a delightful escape into the world of mystery and intrigue.

P.C. James masterfully blends humor, historical accuracy, and engaging storytelling, making him a standout author in cozy mysteries.

> *Kathryn and I were in an online writing group together when we decided to co-author a cozy mystery series. Kathryn writes quilting craft-based cozy mysteries, and we thought a cozy mystery set in England in the Fifties when crafts were still everyday skills would be fun to do. I have a background and an understanding of how people behaved in the social structure of the time. These two different approaches make for difficult plotting sometimes, but the stories are well-received so we get there in the end.*

P.C. James

A Tale of Resilience, Independence, and Storytelling

S. Lee Fisher transitioned from a clinical pharmacist to an award-winning novelist, drawing on her background and personal experiences to create compelling stories featuring strong, independent women.

by Jack Wilson

How a Clinical Pharmacist Became a Multi-Award-Winning Novelist

S. Lee Fisher masterfully blends her professional expertise with creative storytelling, crafting unforgettable narratives that celebrate strong, resilient women.

S. Lee Fisher, also known as Dr. "P.," has made a remarkable transition from a clinical pharmacist to a multi-award-winning fiction writer. Born and raised in small-town Pennsylvania, Fisher's life has been a testament to the strength and independence instilled in her by her mother from an early age. This foundation led her to become the first woman in her county to pay a man support in her mid-twenties, a significant milestone that marked the beginning of her journey as a trailblazer.

After moving to Pittsburgh, Fisher enjoyed a successful corporate career managing retrospective clinical programs for the PBM side of a Fortune 20 company. However, it was the grief of her father's passing that led her to discover a new passion: storytelling. This newfound love for writing, particularly stories featuring strong women, has since become the cornerstone of her career as a novelist.

Fisher's background in pharmacy and her corporate career have significantly influenced her approach to writing and storytelling. She explains, "I have always been left-brain/right-brain equal, with the left having a slight advantage. When choosing a college major, my choices were music, design, or pharmacy. Even as a teen, I knew that I needed money to eat. Pharmacy won." This practical decision laid the groundwork for her structured and organized approach to writing, essential for crafting sweeping generational sagas.

Her corporate experience also taught her the importance of preparation and foresight, skills that have proven invaluable in her writing. "Corporately, I encouraged my staff to prepare not only for the question/task posed but for the next three follow-up questions, which is an applicable approach to writing fiction," Fisher notes.

The theme of strong women is central to Fisher's work, a reflection of her mother's influence. "My mother preached the importance of a woman's independence, both emotional and financial. She never wanted her daughters to be trapped in a marriage or dependent on a man for survival," Fisher recalls. This theme is vividly portrayed in her novels, particularly in "Becoming Olive W." and "Westchester Farm," where her characters navigate the challenges of a time before women could vote, striving for education and independence.

"Becoming Olive W." is set in early 20th century Western Pennsylvania, a historical setting that Fisher meticulously researched to ensure accuracy. "Research is one of my pleasures in life. Canvasing antique stores, rummaging attics, visiting old cemeteries, reenactments, and recreations bring an added dimension to written information," she shares. This dedication to authenticity enriches her storytelling, bringing her characters and their worlds to life.

Fisher's debut novel, "A Mystery of Grace," explores complex themes such as deception, betrayal, and the consequences of decisions. Inspired by her father's memory, Fisher hopes readers understand that actions have consequences, but with contrition, anything is forgivable. "I want my readers to understand that actions suffer consequences, but with contrition, anything is forgivable. However, a little forethought can prevent the need for forgiveness," she emphasizes.

Beyond writing, Fisher's hobbies, including painting watercolors, ballroom dancing, and swimming, also influence her creative process. "I draw on the knowledge of my many hobbies to enhance my characters' attributes," she explains. These personal interests add depth and authenticity to her characters, making them relatable and multifaceted.

For aspiring writers looking to create complex and resilient female characters, Fisher offers valuable advice: "When writing strong women, do not make them successful in all aspects of life. Rather, give them one or two fallible traits to keep them human and relatable." This approach ensures that her characters are not only powerful but also deeply human, with strengths and flaws that resonate with readers.

S. Lee Fisher's journey from pharmacy to fiction is a testament to the power of resilience, passion, and the enduring influence of strong women. Her stories continue to inspire and captivate, offering readers a glimpse into the lives of characters who, much like Fisher herself, navigate life's challenges with strength and grace.

> *I have always been left-brain/right-brain equal, with the left having a slight advantage. When choosing a college major, my choices were music, design, or pharmacy. Even as a teen, I knew that I needed money to eat. Pharmacy won.*

S. Lee Fisher

Literature

Inspires with resilience and self-belief

Joseph Fagarazzi, in an exclusive interview, shares his journey from a troubled childhood to entrepreneurial success, emphasizing resilience, self-belief, and the transformative power of storytelling.

BY JACK WILSON

A Memoir of Triumph and Transformation

Joseph Fagarazzi's life story is one of profound resilience and relentless determination, shaped by early hardships and eventual triumphs across continents and careers. Born on September 7th, 1951, in Venice, Italy, Joseph's childhood was marred by parental neglect and the isolating environment of a convent. At a tender age, he was sent to live in a convent while his parents pursued a new life in London, England. It wasn't until 1960, at the age of nine, that he rejoined his family in London, only to face a cruel and emotionally abusive father who consistently belittled and undermined him.

Despite the challenges and emotional scars inflicted during his formative years, Joseph harbored an unshakable belief in the power of resilience and perseverance. His early struggles instilled in him a drive to prove himself and overcome adversity. This determination became a guiding force throughout his life.

In 1977, Joseph married his Australian wife in a modest ceremony at the Paddington registry office in London. With limited resources but boundless ambition, they embarked on a journey to Australia in 1978, seeking new opportunities and a fresh start. Joseph's entrepreneurial spirit soon led him to manage various clothing stores, where he honed his business acumen and learned the art of customer service.

By 1985, Joseph had established his own clothing store, a venture that grew into a successful chain of three stores over the course of 22 years. Concurrently, he ventured into property development, successfully navigating the market and retaining several units and villas as rental properties to this day. His knack for business and strategic foresight enabled him to diversify his portfolio and secure a stable financial future.

In 2006, Joseph made a pivotal career shift, selling his clothing business to pursue real estate. He earned a Diploma of Property Services and a Certificate IV in Property Services, cementing his expertise in the field. This transition marked a new chapter in his professional journey, one defined by continuous learning and adaptation.

Retirement in 2015 provided Joseph with the opportunity to reconnect with his passions for art and writing. A self-taught artist, he found solace and expression through painting, while his literary pursuits culminated in his memoir, "Escaping My Demons." This deeply personal work chronicles his tumultuous upbringing and the profound impact of childhood trauma on his life. Writing the memoir served as a cathartic process, allowing Joseph to confront and reconcile with his past while offering hope and inspiration to others facing similar challenges.

Through his creative endeavors and candid storytelling, Joseph aims to impart valuable lessons and messages of resilience, self-belief, and the transformative power of personal growth. His journey from an unwanted child in Venice to a respected businessman and author in Australia is a testament to the human spirit's capacity for resilience and reinvention.

Joseph Fagarazzi's experiences in various industries—from retail management to property development—have endowed him with a unique perspective on success and fulfillment. His advice to aspiring entrepreneurs emphasizes the importance of perseverance, integrity, and empathy in navigating challenges and achieving goals. Joseph believes that true success is not solely measured by financial achievements but by the impact one makes in the lives of others and the legacy they leave behind.

Today, Joseph continues to advocate for those affected by childhood trauma, hoping to inspire healing and empowerment through his story. His website, www.josephfagarazziauthor.com, serves as a platform to connect with readers, share insights, and foster a community of resilience and support.

In essence, Joseph Fagarazzi's life is a testament to the enduring power of hope, courage, and resilience in overcoming adversity and finding fulfillment. His journey from hardship to triumph exemplifies the potential for personal growth and transformation, inspiring readers to embrace their own paths with courage and determination.

Joseph Fagarazzi, celebrated author and entrepreneur, shares his journey of overcoming adversity.

> My creative pursuits were monumental in achieving a life of happiness,
>
> Writing my book although it made me relive the past, it also gave me inner peace to move on with my life.
>
> My paintings were a form of rehabilitation or an intermission that kept my mind occupied by not thinking of the past.

Joseph Fagarazzi

MOSAIC DIGEST

Literature

Turning Real-Life Adventures into Riveting Fiction

ROBERT EMMERS

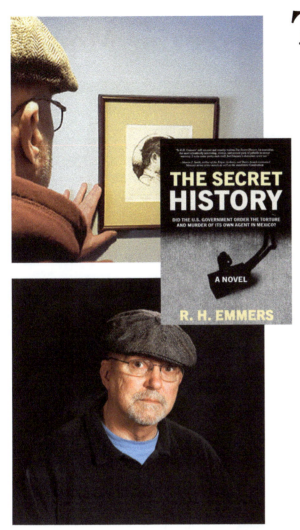

" My life has been an exploration. Probably that's why I've had so many different (and always fun) careers. The idea of exploration carries over into my fiction. "

by Jack Wilson

Robert Emmers, an acclaimed author, has lived a life brimming with extraordinary adventures and experiences that fuel his vivid storytelling. Although he once aspired to write in Paris, Emmers' path led him into journalism, a decision that laid the groundwork for his eclectic career. His professional journey has included roles as a private investigator, insurance fraud detective, and crisis communications specialist. These varied experiences have enriched his fiction, providing a wealth of material drawn from real-life escapades, such as evading federal subpoenas, facing mob threats, and tracking fugitives.

Now residing in the serene woods of northwest Pennsylvania, Emmers has returned to his true passion: writing fiction. His latest works, "The Secret History" and the short story "Where Did All the Dentists Go?", are a testament to his ability to intertwine action-packed narratives with profound existential themes. Emmers' writing is a direct reflection of his adventurous career, combining the thrill of past exploits with the disciplined, concise style honed in the newsroom.

In a revealing interview with Reader's House, Emmers discussed how his diverse professional experiences have shaped his storytelling. He credits his journalism background for his concise writing style, reminiscent of Hemingway. However, he notes that the action and confrontation inherent in his investigative work have profoundly influenced his fiction, ensuring a dynamic and engaging narrative.

"The Secret History" explores themes of government death squads, crime, and vengeance. Emmers explained that the novel originated from his experiences in crisis communication, where he often served as a street-level fixer. Initially an unpublished novel featuring a character named Dahl, the story evolved from a short story set in Mexico—a country Emmers is fond of. The novel's scenes blend his personal experiences with creative imagination.

The short story "Where Did All the Dentists Go?" began with a compelling first line that transformed into a narrative inspired by the Japanese phenomenon of johatsu, where people disappear to start new lives. Emmers emphasizes that he doesn't consciously focus on themes, but a recurring motif in his work is the idea of constant movement and evasion.

Emmers sees parallels between his protagonists' quests for answers and his own journey as a writer. His varied careers mirror the explorative nature of his characters, who are always in search of something. In "The Secret History," the characters, though flawed, are intriguing due to their relentless pursuit of answers.

When it comes to balancing intricate plots with existential themes, Emmers prefers the freedom of short stories, which allow for spontaneous narrative development. He finds the novel-writing process more structured and meticulous, often requiring detailed outlines that may evolve as characters take control. His favorite theme in novels is seeking redemption and moving forward.

Emmers is particularly drawn to unconventional settings and characters, often writing about drunks, misfits, and people in bizarre situations. This fascination stems from the contrast with his relatively conventional life as a writer. Through his characters, he explores worlds far removed from his own, creating immersive and compelling fictional realms. Writing allows him to escape his desk-bound reality and inhabit the lives of crooks and eccentrics.

Whether set in the perilous streets of Mexico or a mysterious village, Robert Emmers' stories offer readers a blend of action, intrigue, and existential exploration. His ability to draw from his adventurous past and infuse it with imagination makes his fiction both gripping and thought-provoking. As he continues to write, Emmers invites readers to embark on journeys filled with excitement and discovery.

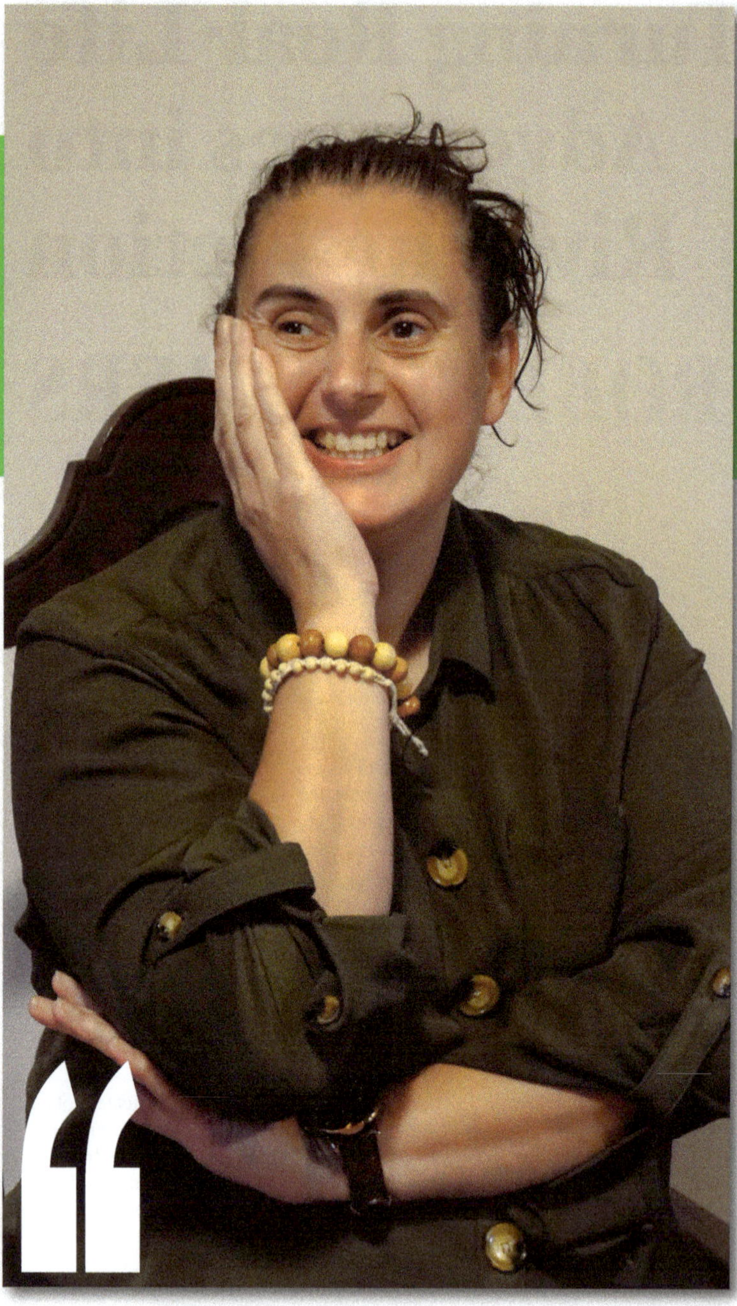

Freezing Moments

Rachael Blakey discusses her transition from drawing to photography, her fascination with time and the macro world, and how her work has been recognized by prestigious outlets like National Geographic.

RACHAEL BLAKEY

The Story Behind "Eye Drops"

as told to Archie Preston

Rachael Blakey, capturing the world through her lens, reveals the hidden beauty in everyday moments with her unique artistic vision.

Art & Photography

Rachael Blakey is a visionary photographer whose journey from the United Kingdom to Canada has been marked by a profound love for art and an exceptional talent for capturing the world through her lens. Her work is a testament to her ability to transform the ordinary into the extraordinary, revealing the hidden beauty in everyday moments. Rachael's photography is not just about capturing images; it's about telling stories and exploring the intricate relationship between time and the environment. Her unique perspective has earned her recognition from prestigious outlets such as National Geographic, where she was awarded the National Geographic Feature Editors' Spotlight in 2019. Her work has also been featured by the BBC, CBC, and Canon (UK) Ltd., showcasing her versatility and skill in capturing a wide variety of subjects.

Rachael's artistic journey began with pencil drawings, a foundation that has deeply influenced her approach to photography. Her ability to see the world differently, honed through years of drawing, allows her to use her camera as a paintbrush, creating visual narratives that evoke emotion and thought. Her acclaimed photograph "Eye Drops," recognized by National Geographic, exemplifies her fascination with the macro world and her talent for revealing what is often hidden from the human eye. Rachael's work is a celebration of the fleeting nature of time, capturing moments that will never happen again and preserving them for eternity. Her dedication to her craft and her continuous pursuit of creative excellence make her a true artist and a remarkable storyteller. You can explore more of Rachael's

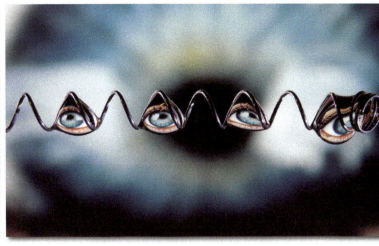

"Take a Breath, Take a Step" by Rachael Blakey: A captivating portrayal of life's journey, this image invites viewers to pause and reflect on the beauty of each moment.

"Eye Drops" by Rachael Blakey: A mesmerizing exploration of the macro world, this photograph reveals hidden reflections, earning multiple recognitions from National Geographic for its innovative perspective and artistic brilliance.

captivating work on her website, www.rachaelskyphotography.com, and her Instagram, @rachaelb321.

Rachael, you started your creative journey as a pencil artist before transitioning to photography. How did this shift come about, and how does your background in drawing influence your approach to photography?

I found the relationship between drawing and photography have a strong connection. I am a visual story teller when I draw and learned to see things around me differently. It was a great way for me to transition to photography because when you draw you are learning about composition and light. I was particularly intrigued by shadows and how the light interacted with shapes around it. I want to convey a message with my photography, a visual representation of an idea, mood or emotion. With the skills I learned from my artwork, I can now use my camera as a paintbrush to paint the environment around me.

Your work, such as the "Eye Drops" photograph, has been recognized multiple times by National Geographic. Can you share the story behind this image and what it means to you personally and artistically?

I am honoured and humbled for the recognition from the National Geographic for my work titled "Eye Drops". I am fascinated with the macro world that is hidden from human eyes. My goal with that particular photograph was to reveal what was hidden from people's eyes, and in fact what was hidden were eyes reflected in water drops that I had carefully placed onto a metal spring. The title of the photograph is also a play on words. This photograph has recently found a home and is hanging on the wall of the IWK Hospital specialist eye clinic in Halifax, Nova Scotia, Canada.

You describe your photography as an "exploration of time" and its relationship with the environment. Could you elaborate on how time plays a role in your work, and how you capture that sense of temporality in your photographs?

I do see my photography as an exploration of time. The moment you take a photograph, that split second, that emotion, laugh, smile, tears or a gaze you capture will never happen again. As a photographer you can freeze that moment and preserve it. I find this particularly important when I am capturing people's portraits, even more so when clients have asked me to do their photographs of loved ones who were ill. Being a photographer has also taught me to respect time, and realise how temporary certain things can be. Time is a journey and photography can freeze that journey and transport you to different places when you look at photographs.

With your work being published in prestigious outlets like National Geographic, BBC News, and featured in international exhibitions, how do you feel these opportunities have shaped your career and artistic growth?

I am very grateful and humble to be published and featured with various organizations. Having my work exhibited in Manhattan, New York was a dream come true for me. It has certainly increased my confidence as a photographer, but I am still quite self critical of my work. I always think it could be better, so I tend to push myself more creatively to come up with new ideas or different ways to photograph subjects.

As someone who specializes in Creative Fine Art Photography, what inspires your compositions, and how do you approach balancing creativity with technical precision in your pieces?

Trying to balance the creativity side of things with technical precision I find takes patience and a lot of trial and error. Finding a balance that allows my imagination to run without compromising the technical side of things requires continuous learning and the need to always want to do better.

An example of finding this balance between being creative and technical can be found with my photography series titled "Through a Rainy Window". Through a Rainy Window, depicts street photography taken through windows with rain on. I enjoy capturing the play of light in the rain, the reflections of buildings and vehicles. The intrinsic nature of everyday life captured in the rain. But I find it challenging because of the environment I am working in, the rain.

I have also been able to find a balance with my photography due to having arthritis in both of my hands and both feet, which has actually made me even more driven and passionate about my photography.

> Rachael Blakey masterfully transforms ordinary moments into extraordinary art, capturing the essence of time with unparalleled creativity and vision.

Exploring the Intersections

Januario Jano discusses his interdisciplinary art practice, exploring identity and cultural narratives, and his commitment to social engagement through initiatives like Pés Descalços and TEDxLuanda, fostering cultural dialogue and innovation.

JANUARIO JANO
Artistic Journey Through Identity and Culture

as told to Archie Preston

Januario Jano stands as a beacon of innovation and cultural introspection in the contemporary art world. His interdisciplinary approach, spanning sculpture, video, photography, textile, sound installation, and performance, reflects a profound commitment to exploring the intricate balance between fiction and reality. With a Master's Degree in Fine Arts from Goldsmiths University in London, Jano's work is deeply rooted in research, allowing him to delve into complex themes of identity, home, and cultural narratives. His art challenges both historic and contemporary narratives, offering a fresh perspective on the interconnectedness of global cultures and economies.

Jano's contributions extend beyond the canvas, as he actively engages in cultural and social initiatives. He founded Pés Descalços, a collective dedicated to promoting artistic and cultural projects in Angola, and has been instrumental in launching TEDxLuanda, fostering dialogue and innovation in a country emerging from its tumultuous past. His work has been exhibited internationally, earning a place in prestigious private and public collections. Januario Jano's art not only captivates with its aesthetic depth but also serves as a catalyst for cultural development and social transformation, making him a pivotal figure in the global art scene.

Your work spans a wide range of mediums, from sculpture to video and sound installations. How do you decide which medium best serves a particular idea, and how do these various forms of expression complement one another in your practice?

The research phase offers both a grounding foundation and a sense of openness to unexpected shifts. It can serve as a point of departure, facilitate and clarify the core themes or ideas I want to explore, but at the same time, it leaves room for those

Januario Jano, the visionary artist, in his studio, where he crafts thought-provoking works that challenge cultural narratives and inspire dialogue.

Art & Photography

ideas to evolve or take new forms as I engage with the materials. The research can lead to moments of surprise, pushing me to approach the project from angles I hadn't anticipated.

As for the relationship between different mediums, it seems they complement each other in practice. Some mediums may provide a tactile, immediate connection to the materials, while others mediums offer a more fluid, temporal space to work within. The interplay between these mediums enhances the overall depth of the work, as each medium can push the boundaries of how I communicate an idea.

Much of your work explores the delicate balance between fiction and reality, especially in relation to identity and cultural narratives. How do you approach this balance, and what role does it play in shaping your perspective on contemporary issues?

The balance between fiction and reality in my work speaks to the complex layers of identity and cultural narratives that fused my interest in exploring themes such as; personal and cultural identity, and

> Januario Jano is a visionary artist whose work transcends boundaries, inspiring cultural dialogue and transformation through innovative, interdisciplinary art.

cultural production, which are often fluid and multifaceted. These topics, I likely aim to challenge perceptions of what is "true" or "authentic" in the stories we tell or hear about ourselves and our cultures. This tension between the two realms becomes a way to question not just personal identity, but the structure of the social fabric, especially as they relate to issues of representation, history, and power dynamics.

Approaching this balance may require an exploration of both the subjective experience and external realities — recognising how identity is shaped by the interplay of cultural histories, myths, and individual experiences. Fiction allows a space for reimagining or reframing reality, and that can be elementary in addressing contemporary issues such as migration, globalisation, or the way marginalised communities are often portrayed.

Your projects often challenge both historic and contemporary narratives within the context of globalisation. How do you use your art to critique or reflect on the cultural interdependence and evolving identities brought about by this global interconnectedness?

Exploring both historic and contemporary narratives through the lens of globalisation allows me to address the complexities of cultural interdependence and evolving identities. In an increasingly interconnected world, the blending of cultures, economies, and technologies creates new spaces for dialogue but also raises questions of power, ownership, and identity. Through my practice, I can critique the ways globalisation impacts these areas — from the erasure of local identities to the homogenization of cultures, and the unequal exchange of resources and influence.

By using various mediums, I likely engage with this interdependence in both abstract and tangible ways. Sculpture, video, textile, performance or sound installations can offer a physical manifestation of these cultural flows, creating spaces where different histories and narratives collide, merge, or contrast. Your art becomes a platform to reflect on how globalisation reshapes our understanding of self and other, exposing the ways identities are constructed, deconstructed, and recontextualized in this global context.

You've been a driving force in cultural initiatives like Pés Descalços and TEDxLuanda. How do these philanthropic and social engagement projects intersect with your artistic practice, and what do you see as the role of the artist in fostering cultural development?

Pés Descalços started as I felt the need to engaged and contribute to the local cultural and artistic landscape outside my own practice, it feels the existent gap between me and the society in a large context as TEDxLuanda, these cultural initiatives are parallel to my artistic practice in fostering community, dialogue, and engagement with cultural narratives. These initiatives likely create platforms for voices that are often underrepresented, offering a space for conversations about identity, heritage, and the

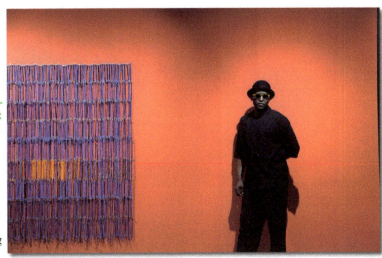

Januario Jano at his solo exhibition "Butaiuri" in Tokyo, where his innovative works invite viewers to explore themes of identity and cultural interconnectedness.

impact of globalisation, themes that are also central to my art practice.

By intersecting philanthropic work with my creative practice, I often embody the idea that art isn't just about self-expression but can be a tool for cultural development and social transformation. I see the artist as both a creator and a facilitator, someone who bridges diverse perspectives, encouraging collective reflection, social development and critical thinking.

Research is a core element of your practice. Can you share more about your research process and how it informs the conceptual and material choices in your work, particularly when dealing with themes of identity and home?

My research process likely plays a pivotal role in shaping both the conceptual framework and the material execution of your work. When dealing with themes like identity and home, the research might involve delving into historical narratives, personal stories, cultural identity and production. This multidisciplinary approach allows me to uncover layers of meaning that can inform not only the direction of the project but also the mediums I choose to work with.

For instance, if you're exploring the notion of home, my research might focus on the architectural, emotional, and cultural dimensions of space — which could influence whether I decide to represent these ideas through textile base work, sculpture, performance, video, photography, installation, or sound.

Similarly, when grappling with identity, the research could extend into areas like post-colonial theory, displacement, or oral histories, offering a rich context that informs the final decisions of the project in hand.

In your artist statement, you emphasise the role of the body and its multidimensional representation in your work. How do you explore the body's relationship with space, culture, and history, and how does this theme manifest across different projects?

The body in my work plays a pivotal role, it acts as a symbol, representing the intersection of space, culture, and history. It carries cultural memory, political meaning, and personal narratives, serving as a site where history and identity are negotiated and contested.

In relation to space, the body can explore themes of belonging and displacement, symbolising movement or transition, especially in the context of globalisation or migration. Culturally, it reflects how identity is constructed and performed through race, gender, and heritage.

This theme appears across my projects in different ways — from physicality in sculpture or performance to absence or fragmentation in video, photography, and sound installations.

Discovering Beauty in Layers

Yana Barabash discusses her artistic journey, the influence of the Isle of Wight, her creative process, and her approach to life coaching, emphasizing the importance of finding joy in the present.

YANA BARABASH

Artistic Journey Through Emotion and Nature

as told to Archie Preston

Yana Barabash is a visionary artist whose work transcends the boundaries of traditional painting, capturing the essence of human emotion and the beauty of the natural world. Born in Odessa, Yana's artistic journey began at a young age, and her passion for art has only deepened over the years. Her unique ability to convey complex emotions through her portraits and genre compositions has earned her a well-deserved reputation in the art world. Yana's dedication to her craft is evident in her multi-layered paintings, which invite viewers to explore the intricate details and textures that define her style. Her work is a testament to her belief in the transformative power of art, offering a glimpse into her dreams and the world as she sees it.

In this exclusive interview for Mosaic Digest Magazine, Yana Barabash opens up about her artistic journey, the influences that have shaped her work, and the profound impact of her move to the Isle of Wight. She shares insights into her creative process, revealing how she balances traditional techniques with modern technology to bring her visions to life. Yana also discusses her approach to life coaching, offering a unique perspective on finding joy and fulfillment in the present moment. Her story is one of resilience, passion, and an unwavering commitment to sharing beauty with the world. Join us as we delve into the mind of this extraordinary artist and explore the inspirations behind her captivating works.

How has your experience of moving to the Isle of Wight influenced your artistic style and the themes you explore in your paintings?

When I moved to the Isle of Wight, I was dealing with many

Yana Barabash, a visionary artist, finds inspiration in the serene landscapes of the Isle of Wight.

Art & Painting

life changes, including thoughts about the war, my child's future, and my artistic career. The island provided a much-needed sense of peace and safety. I knew before arriving that it was a beautiful place, and I hoped the stunning landscapes would help distract me from the harsh realities of life. That's exactly what happened—right from the first few days, I began to paint, and I believe that painting is what saved me from falling into a deep depression.

Before coming here, I had never painted so many seascapes, despite being born and raised in Odessa, a city by the sea. But Odessa is a big city with a population nearing a million, and its beaches are more developed, making it hard to find untouched nature.

Now, after almost three years of living on the island, I have so many plans to capture its beautiful hills, cottages, and sheep. The quiet, slow pace of island life gives me the time to reflect and find inspiration. I no longer feel rushed, and my life here is very measured.

If I ever want to immerse myself in culture, there's nothing better than spending a couple of days the white canvas with beige or gray acrylic before starting to paint, as not everyone enjoys painting on pure white.

My painting is multi-layered because the more layers I apply, the more depth I achieve. I also can't imagine my work without details. Since childhood, I've loved studying paintings, discovering new facets, which is what I now strive for in my own work.

What are some of the hidden gems on the Isle of Wight that have inspired your recent works, and how do you capture their essence in your art?

There are many hidden gems on the Isle of Wight that inspire me. I think the main thing I capture and want to showcase is the quintessential English vibe, which I, as a foreigner, feel is more pronounced for me. The old, beautiful walls, cottages, roses, moss, and lush greenery are things that always fascinated me in English films and series. The tides, moss-covered boulders, crabs, slopes, seagulls, and the new-to-me groins and trees growing right out of the water are all sources of inspiration. And who better than me to convey the incredible variety of greenery and textures, given my love for detail?

How do you balance the use of traditional techniques with modern technology, such as sketching on a tablet, in your creative process?

I travel a lot, which is a necessity for me. It refreshes my perspective and brings new discoveries. I used to take an easel and small canvases with me, but now I've realized that the main thing for me in traveling is to observe, see, and live. But when ideas arise, I sketch on my tablet, which is a fast and effective way to capture ideas, and sometimes even finish a piece. However, I always transfer my best ideas to canvas because there's something special about creating something physical with my own hands, covered with my own fingers. It's also a wonderful way to experiment with textures and try different color schemes for the same painting. It really speeds up my process.

Can you tell me more about your approach to life coaching and how it can help someone achieve their personal goals?

Life coaching is incredibly help-

Yana Barabash's multi-layered paintings reveal intricate details and textures, capturing the essence of human emotion and natural beauty.

ful, though in my case, my knowledge has come from experience. I believe it's important to understand what brings us happiness and joy, both for ourselves and for others. The war has taught us to live in the moment, to appreciate what we have, to not dwell on small problems, and not to plan too far ahead. Oddly enough, we've learned to find joy in every day.

Just recently, I was back home in Odessa, and I was struck by how people were living—they were sitting in cafes, swimming in the sea, enjoying life to the fullest, and that's the right approach. We can't cry and grieve all the time.

> Yana Barabash masterfully captures human emotion and nature's beauty, creating multi-layered paintings that invite viewers into her visionary world.

in London. It's a city that offers everything—exhibitions, museums, social connections, and my beloved Argentine tango, which I've been dancing for many years.

Can you describe your process of creating a multi-layered painting and how you decide which textures and details to incorporate?

A few years ago, I discovered a way to speed up my painting process. I'm a fan of oil painting, as I believe no other technique achieves the same depth and detail. But the major drawback of oil painting is the drying time of the layers. Now, I start with acrylics, often freely and in a watercolor style, getting as much done with acrylics as possible, and then finish the final details with oils. Acrylic also serves as an excellent base for oil paint. Back in my student days, we often coated

Memory and Emotion

Yana Barabash discusses her artistic journey, the influence of the Isle of Wight, her creative process, and her approach to life coaching, emphasizing the importance of finding joy in the present.

SOFIA RUIZ

Exploring the Boundaries of Creativity and Self-Discovery

"A Soft Spot" by Sofia Ruíz, 2024. This captivating oil and acrylic piece on canvas (76.2 x 101.6 cm) invites viewers to explore the delicate interplay of color and emotion.

as told to Jenny Taylor

Sofia Ruiz stands as a beacon of artistic innovation and cultural exploration, her work resonating deeply with audiences around the globe. Born in San José, Costa Rica, Sofia embarked on her artistic journey at the tender age of 16, driven by a profound sense of isolation and a longing for connection. Her early experiences, marked by personal challenges, have profoundly shaped her creative vision, infusing her art with themes of psychoanalysis, duality, and memory. With a degree in Painting and Printmaking from the School of Fine Arts in Costa Rica and a Master's in Education, Sofia has not only honed her craft but also enriched her understanding of art as a medium for communication and healing. Her impressive portfolio includes over 35 exhibitions worldwide and participation in international residencies from the USA to South Korea, each experience adding a unique layer to her artistic narrative. Sofia's work is a visual diary that explores identity and the influence of family, offering viewers a chance to reflect on their own emotional landscapes. Her accolades, including several national and international art awards, underscore her impact and dedication to her craft.

In this exclusive interview for Mosaic Digest Magazine, Sofia Ruiz opens up about her artistic journey, the interplay between painting and printmaking in her work, and the cultural influences that have shaped her thematic focus. She

Art & Painting

A Soft Spot Oil and Acrylic on canvas
76,2 x 101,6 cm 2024

The Aloof Artist_Oil on canvas
61 x 61 cm_2024

LadyBird_oil on canvas
61 x 61 cm_

shares insights into the significant moments of her career, the role of education in her artistic practice, and the universal messages she hopes to convey through her art. Join us as we delve into the mind

> Sofia Ruiz masterfully blends emotion and technique, creating art that resonates universally and inspires introspection across cultural boundaries.

of this extraordinary artist, whose work continues to inspire and connect people across diverse cultural contexts.

Your journey as an artist began at the age of 16 in San José, Costa Rica. What initially drew you to the world of art, and how did those early experiences shape your style and creative vision?

I started drawing at five because my father gave me small notebooks and a pen to keep me occupied while we waited to see my mother. She suffered from temporary amnesia for a few years, and I think that, along with the lack of photographs from my childhood, influenced me significantly. During that time, I felt disconnected from my family; my mother didn't recognize me, and my father was often working. Those feelings of isolation and longing for connection became integral to my artistic drive.

At 16, I began looking for art through tattoo magazines and tried to copy designs, and I realized that drawing came naturally to me. As I grew, art helped me find the sense of belonging I was missing. These experiences sparked my interest in psychoanalysis, duality, and memory, which later shaped my creative vision. My work has become a visual diary exploring my identity and how family influences who we are. It's also a healing process that continues to evolve.

In 2007, you majored in Painting and Printmaking from the School of Fine Arts in Costa Rica. How do these mediums complement each other in your work, and what influences your choice between them for different projects?

Printmaking offers many techniques and materials to explore. I appreciate the complexity of processes like etching, which involve trial and error. Painting, on the other hand, allows for spontaneity and immediate expression. Working in both mediums has taught me to balance exploration with the freedom that painting offers.

When I want to layer ideas carefully, I choose printmaking. But when I want to express something raw and intuitive, I turn to painting. These two mediums complement each other, allowing me to maintain a dynamic creative process between structure and freedom.

You have participated in international residencies from the USA to South Korea. How have these experiences in different cultures influenced your artistic process and thematic focus?

Each residency has broadened my understanding of how art operates in different cultural contexts. Some exposed me to new ways of blending technology with traditional printmaking, encouraging experimentation. Engaging with artists from diverse backgrounds has been particularly enriching because you can see how our cultures influence how we view things through a different lens.

As an award-winning artist with over 35 exhibitions globally, what do you consider the most significant moments in your career so far, and how have they impacted your approach to art?

A meaningful moment was my first solo exhibition, where I felt both excited and exposed.

Every opportunity to show my work feels significant, whether in a small gallery or a museum. In Costa Rica, opportunities can feel limited, so seeing my work appreciated abroad has been incredibly rewarding.

Winning the Best Overseas Artist Prize at the Women in Art Prize in London was another important moment. These experiences have helped build my confidence to continue creating, even in challenging times.

In addition to your artistic practice, you hold a Master's in Education. How has your background in education influenced the way you engage with your work, and do you see a connection between teaching and creating?

Teaching has helped me simplify complex ideas, which influences my art. Both art and teaching involve breaking down intricate concepts like identity into relatable expressions, facilitating a deeper connection with the viewer. Both teaching and creating are ways of understanding and sharing ideas, helping me express them in a clearer, more accessible way.

What message or emotion do you hope viewers take away from your work, especially considering the diverse cultural contexts you engage with in your exhibitions around the world?

I hope viewers feel a sense of introspection when they engage with my work. I often explore themes of fragmentation, identity, and memory, and I want people to leave with a deeper understanding of their emotional layers. The ultimate message is that our experiences, though complex and fragmented, leave traces that connect us all. I explore the duality of identity: how we define ourselves versus how others perceive us. This theme resonates universally, regardless of cultural context.

THE COVER CONVERSATION

> "Janet Hennessey Dilenschneider brings her unique perspective to life, creating serene landscapes that encourage a deeper connection with the environment.

Painting Hope and Harmony

JANET HENNESSEY DILENSCHNEIDER

How Nature and Expressionism Shape Her Visionary Art

as told to Hazel Ivy

> *"Janet Hennessey Dilenschneider, an expressionist painter, draws inspiration from nature to create serene landscapes. Her work emphasizes hope and beauty, encouraging viewers to connect with art and environmental issues."*

In the world of contemporary art, few artists capture the ethereal beauty and profound serenity of nature quite like Janet Hennessey Dilenschneider. From her early beginnings, when a chance encounter with the legendary Roy Lichtenstein set her on a path of artistic discovery, to her current status as a celebrated expressionist painter, Dilenschneider's journey is as inspiring as her work. Her paintings, characterized by rich palettes, loose brush strokes, and luminous misty vistas, invite viewers to experience the world through her eyes—where light and color dance in harmonious symphony.

Mosaic Digest magazine is proud to feature Janet Hennessey Dilenschneider on our cover, celebrating her unique ability to convey hope and tranquility through her art. Her latest exhibition, "Come To The Light," is a testament to her commitment to providing peace and solace in a troubled world. By drawing inspiration from the natural beauty of her Connecticut surroundings and the broader global landscape, Dilenschneider's work resonates with a universal message of renewal and inspiration.

In this exclusive interview, we delve into the creative process behind her evocative landscapes, her influences from impressionism and expressionism, and her dedication to using art as a medium for social commentary. As she continues to evolve and explore new themes, Janet Hennessey Dilenschneider remains a beacon of artistic innovation and a testament to the transformative power of art. Join us as we explore the mind and heart of an artist who invites us all to fall in love with nature—and ourselves—all over again. Your exhibition Come To The Light emphasizes the serenity and beauty of nature.

Can you share more about your creative process and how your surroundings in Connecticut influence your work?

My surroundings PLUS what is happening in the world GREATLY affects my paintings. With "Come To The Light" my objective is to give PEACE and SOLACE to a troubled world… thus, to give INSPIRATION and HOPE.

When, one very early morning, I passed a second-floor window and saw the beautiful sunrise, I was impressed beyond belief and

Continued *on page 20*

Continued *from page 19*

THE COVER CONVERSATION

SPRING TREES, 24 X 30

A vibrant celebration of renewal, this painting captures the essence of spring with its lively colors and dynamic composition, inviting viewers to experience the rejuvenating energy of nature's awakening.

motivated to paint that sunrise. I then thought, this is the THEME of the show. I followed with mostly paintings which had lovely reflections of sun on water or giving highlights to some object. Light and sun are inspiring to many people, even spiritual to some.

You had a memorable encounter with Roy Lichtenstein early in your career. How did that experience shape your journey as an artist, and are there any other pivotal moments that have influenced your artistic path?

Yes, at about 16, I entered a painting in a formal juried show, for the first time. Initially, I was rejected and very disappointed. A man offered to help me by putting the required hanging wires on the back. I subsequently learned it was Roy Lichtenstein and the curator of the show. Later a friend called and said I had won first place in Water Color. How motivating!

Other moments were when a teacher in an art class pulled me aside and suggested I major in art. It seemed so obvious then.

One of the most professionally motivating moments was when an important gallery owner in Paris that we had just had dinner with looked at my work on a CD and said, "Well, I guess we are just going to have to give you a show" … my first SOLO show and in Paris! That was 2013 and I have had 14 solo shows since them, 7 as a result of my Paris gallery exhibition.

The title of your exhibition, "Come To The Light," suggests a sense of hope and tranquility. What message or emotions do you hope to convey to viewers through this collection of paintings?

I want whomever needs a little "hope" or reinforcement to get the spiritual feeling from the paintings and allow themselves to feel a sense of renewal. Art can be healing and motivational if we allow it to be.

As an artist, I have a personal obligation to give something to my viewer. My objective is to

Surrounded by her vibrant landscapes, Janet Hennessey Dilenschneider finds inspiration in the natural world to create art that speaks to the soul.

THE COVER CONVERSATION

ROAD THROUGH PROVENCE, 24 X 36

This captivating piece transports viewers to the sun-drenched landscapes of Provence, where winding roads lead through fields of color and light, capturing the serene beauty and timeless charm of the region.

GLORIOUS SUNSET, OIL ON CANVAS, 24 X 30

This stunning painting captures the breathtaking beauty of a sunset, with vibrant hues and masterful brushwork that evoke the warmth and tranquility of the day's end.

have them participate in the painting and get something out of it.

You are known for your expressionist style with influences from impressionism. Can you discuss how these styles have impacted your work and how you have developed your unique artistic voice over the years?

As an Expressionist painter, I want you to FEEL what I feel and like about that tree. How do I attempt to do this? I use very free brushstrokes, if the strokes are angled and deftly put down, they are to me the PASSION in the painting. This PASSION is shown through the GESTURE lines and colors laid down next to each other.

The color is the JOY, not just one color but the combination of colors. One color can "modify" how you see the other – they add excitement. They "sing" together as I like to say. This is called "simultaneous contrast," and it is often used today. It is, however, revered and borrowed from the Impressionists, that and their freedom of stroke are the two greatest concepts they gave us. They freed up the way for Abstract Expressionists and today's contemporary artists.

With several exhibitions planned for later this year, can you give us a glimpse into what you are working on next and any new themes or ideas you are excited to explore in your upcoming projects?

I am currently working on new techniques and subject matter. An artist needs to constantly evolve and challenge their own artistry and bring it to new heights. I am in love with the shapes of clouds and "misting out" landscape scenes.

You mentioned that your passion for the arts was "inherited" from your mother and sister. How did their influence shape your artistic style and career, and are there specific lessons or techniques you learned from them that you still use today?

I was surrounded with art as a youngster. My mother's paintings were very realistic. If I were her art teacher, I would have suggested she "free up" her brushstroke, however, her colors were beautiful. I still remember sitting at the breakfast table as a young girl with my sister and she told us, "Always put your lightest lights next to your darkest darks." I do use this technique today, and I also use it as a philosophy of life.

You've expressed a desire for artists to comment on societal issues, particularly ecology and global warming. How do you balance conveying a message about these critical issues while also creating art that provides a sense of peace and beauty?

Janet Hennessey Dilenschneider brings her unique perspective to life, creating serene landscapes that encourage a deeper connection with the environment.

Continued *on page 22*

MOSAIC DIGEST || 21

THE COVER CONVERSATION

Continued *from page 21*

Good question. I do believe artists have the right, even the obligation, to make reference to social change.

I try to get the viewer to "Participate" in the painting and see the point of view I have about the issue. In my first solo shows, I wanted to have the viewer "fall in love with nature all over again" as I like to say. My goal was to develop an awareness of the ecology.

I showed beautiful trees, greenery and leaves which everyone could appreciate. Now, recently I have tried to get the viewer to feel that sense of calm and renewal which the "Come To The Light" Exhibition has shown.

I do believe a painting can affect a person. The way I reflect ecology, global warming, and conflict in the world that causes unrest is to treat the subjects with calming and beautiful images. Beauty in the art is what does the work.

Can you elaborate on your creative process, particularly how you let your "creative brain" take over when interpreting colors and designs? How do experiences, like your drive through Provence, influence your work?

The "Creative Process" is many things: very easy, complicated and interpretive. I always look at all visual stimuli, specially if I am looking for something to "spark" a painting. I try to never copy but as many famous artists have said, "let the paint take you and tell you where to go." This is where your "creative brain" should take over. You have been sending artistic messages and images to your "artistic brain" for a long time. Now you work on your painting and look for the "newness" you want to create.

My ride through Provence was a perfect example. There were many beautiful treelined allées and I had the driver stop at least 8 times to photograph them. I was enchanted with the scenes, the colors, shadows, and winding roads. Five paintings were the result. None are exactly alike in color or style. This was one of my "Creative Brain" escapades.

> *Janet H. Dilenschneider's masterful use of color and light creates a breathtaking vista that stretches beyond the canvas, symbolizing infinite possibilities.*

SUNRISE, COME TO THE LIGHT, 36 X 48

Janet's evocative painting invites viewers to embrace the dawn's first light, with its radiant colors and dynamic composition symbolizing hope and new beginnings.

THE COVER CONVERSATION

GREEN RUSHES INTO YELLOW GRASSES, 30 X 30

Janet's vibrant painting beautifully captures the interplay of nature's colors, where lilac reflections blend into golden grasses, evoking a sense of calm and excitement to the color contrast.

You've had the opportunity to do solo exhibitions in various locations. How does the freedom to paint what you feel and see impact your work, and are there any particular themes or subjects you are eager to explore in future exhibitions?

What one "feels" about what one sees is what it is all about. If you don't have a feeling about the scene, go to the next scene. Right now, I am into CLOUDS and how to paint them with a "misty" look. They are magical. I am also in love with ATMOSPHERE and how it is shimmery and misty with one color blending into another. That is where I am going now with my brush. There is a lot of violence in the world today. I won't paint THAT! I want people to be uplifted and enlightened, I paint the "Light" not the "Dark."

You advise young painters to "beat their own drum" and "observe, observe, observe." Can you share more about how emerging artists can find their unique voice and the importance of being attuned to the world around them in their creative journey?

I always advise young artists to LOOK at everything they can: art books of favorite artists, art magazines, galleries, museums. Spend some time learning about what others have done. Spend some good time on this and then do your personal research. Look at the different shapes of leaves in a garden, or of clouds floating by, or colors next to each other in a flower garden. Then let your "Creative Brain" take over. Always remember GESTURE which is Design of the piece and COLOR which is the biggest attraction .... and the JOY.

The Chinese artists say, "Draw it 9 times; paint it once." Try that too **End**

Literature

Exploring the Journey

Thomas White's diverse career spans acting, directing, and writing. His novels, inspired by historical events and personal experiences, captivate readers with imaginative storytelling and emotional depth.

as told to J. Evans

Master Storyteller Across Mediums

Thomas White's journey from the theater to the literary world is a testament to the power of storytelling in all its forms. Beginning his career as an actor, White quickly transitioned to directing, earning accolades such as Drama-Logue and Critics awards. His role as Artistic Director for a Los Angeles theater set the stage for his future endeavors, including the world tour of *"The Teenage Mutant Ninja Turtles: Coming Out Of Their Shells,"* which captivated nearly a million children worldwide. With a career spanning over two decades as President and Creative Director of Maiden Lane Entertainment, White has orchestrated large-scale corporate events for giants like Harley Davidson and Microsoft. Now, as an acclaimed author, he continues to weave compelling narratives, with his latest novel, "The Edison Enigma," adding to his growing literary repertoire.

White's diverse background in theater and event production has profoundly influenced his approach to writing. "*As a director, you tell stories using actors, sets, props, and lighting. As an author, you use your words,*" he explains. This seamless transition from stage to page underscores his belief that the core objective remains the same: to engage the audience emotionally. Whether through a theatrical production or a novel, White's goal is to captivate and entertain, ensuring that the audience remains invested from beginning to end.

The Edison Enigma, White's third novel, delves into the intriguing concept of time travel and the consequences of altering history. The inspiration for this theme came from a corporate event for Saturn in 1997, where the electric car, the EV-1, was unveiled. Years later, an article titled "The Death Of The Electric Car" sparked White's curiosity about the historical trajectory of electric vehicles. His research revealed a series of coincidences at the turn of the 20th century, leading him to imagine a scenario where the world chose electric cars over internal combustion engines. This imaginative leap forms the crux of *The Edison Enigma,* blending science fiction with historical speculation to create a thought-provoking narrative.

In *The Siren's Scream,* White explores the eerie Thornton Mansion and its mysterious tide pool, a setting that exudes suspense and dread. Initially inspired by mermaid myths, White sought to breathe new life into the well-worn trope. The idea of mermaids dealing with familial conflicts and lineage sparked a storyline that evolved into a gripping tale of mystery and intrigue. By reimagining the mermaid mythos, White crafted a novel that stands out in the genre, offering readers a fresh perspective on an ancient legend.

Justice Rules, White's debut novel, centers on FBI Special Agent Brian Wylie and a vigilante coalition. The plot was inspired by the aftermath of the OJ Simpson trial, particularly the emotional devastation of Ron Goldman's father, Fred. This poignant moment led White to ponder the lengths one might go to seek justice outside the legal system. The resulting narrative explores themes of justice and morality, challenging readers to consider the complexities of revenge and retribution.

Recognition as a finalist in the Pacific Northwest Writers Association 2010 Literary contest for "Justice Rules" was a significant milestone in White's writing career. Although he did not immediately follow up with another novel, the nomination affirmed his talent and potential as a writer. Reflecting on the experience, White acknowledges the honour but also the overwhelming nature of his accomplishment, which led to a decade-long hiatus before his next literary endeavor.

Balancing the creative demands of writing novels with the logistical challenges of producing events is no small feat, yet White finds parallels between the two processes. "*I always describe my career as being someone in production,*" he says. Whether producing plays, corporate events, or novels, the skill set remains consistent: envisioning a project and bringing it to life. The blank page, much like an empty stage, represents both a challenge and an opportunity for creativity to flourish.

Thomas White's multifaceted career exemplifies the versatility and resilience of a true storyteller. From the theater to the corporate world and now to the realm of literature, his ability to engage and entertain remains unwavering. As he continues to craft new narratives, readers can look forward to more captivating tales from this accomplished author.

Thomas White's storytelling prowess and creative versatility make him a standout author, seamlessly blending history, imagination, and emotion.

> " *I always describe my career as being someone in production. I produce plays, musicals, sales events, corporate meetings, product reveals, novels, etc. The skill set is pretty much the same, you create a vision in your head, then utilize your skill set to make it come to life. Writer's always talk about the blank piece of paper and how there is nothing scarier. That is 100% true.*

Thomas White

Literature

Why Financial Planning Is a Great Career Option for Women

Financial planning is an increasingly popular and lucrative career for women, offering high salaries, work-life balance, personal fulfillment, and strong support networks, including initiatives, scholarships, and mentorships from the CFP Board.

as told to J. Evans

Financial planning was once thought of as a male-dominated industry, but that's quickly changing. The number of women getting their CERTIFIED FINANCIAL PLANNER™ certification is growing year over year — and for good reason: The benefits of entering this field as a woman are numerous. Below are a few to consider.

• It's lucrative. Financial planners are in high demand and are well-compensated for their expertise. A financial advisor can pull in a generous salary right out of the gate, and earning the right credentials can boost compensation significantly. The median income for those with CFP® certification and less than 5 years of experience is $100,000 — and that median figure grows to $206,000 with 10 or more years of experience. In general, financial advisors with CFP® certification earn 12% more than those without.

• Being a CFP® professional offers good work-life balance. With the potential to work remotely and create one's own schedule, financial planning is a career path well-suited to those looking for flexibility and a desirable work-life balance.

• Financial planning can be personally fulfilling. Providing competent, ethical financial advice that helps others achieve their life goals — from sending their children to college to securing a comfortable retirement — can be extremely gratifying.

Research also finds that female CFP® professionals have a unique dedication to providing holistic financial planning. Working as a financial planner provides opportunities to uplift and empower other women, as well as members of groups historically given fewer opportunities to accumulate wealth.

• Women who aspire to become CFP® professionals will find support in many places. CFP Board, for example, has implemented initiatives to recruit women and advance their careers.

Some firms subsidize the cost of CFP® certification and give employees time away from work to study for the CFP® exam. Additionally, women's networks and business councils can help build leadership skills and professional confidence, and many firms are even paying their employees' membership fees.

CFP Board also administers scholarships for individuals underrepresented in the field, along with a mentoring program.

To learn more and get started today on your path to becoming a CFP® professional, visit getCFPcertified.org.

With demand for personal financial advisors expected to grow significantly in the coming years, and the industry making way for more women professionals, it's worth exploring this rewarding career path.

PHOTO SOURCE: monkeybusinessimages / iStock via Getty Images Plus (StatePoint)

Literature

Crafting Empathy and Environmental Awareness in 'Panda Demick'

John Shay's "Panda Demick" uses a talking panda to explain the pandemic and environmental crises, emphasizing empathy, family connections, and nature's balance, inspired by his grandson's birth during COVID-19.

by S. Roberts

John Shay, a retired Earth scientist and high-tech entrepreneur, resides in Seattle, Washington, with his oceanographer wife, Joan. With degrees in chemistry and geophysics, John has had a remarkable career, including spearheading the landmark BBC World News Hong Kong Handover Internet Cybercast in 1997 and overseeing the first live cybercasting of a World Cup finals match in 1998. Today, he dedicates his time to rebuilding a century-old farmhouse near Lake Washington. The birth of his grandson during the early days of the COVID-19 pandemic inspired him to write "Panda Demick," a story that intertwines the pandemic with broader environmental themes.

The arrival of John's grandson on March 13, 2020, just days after the World Health Organization declared COVID-19 a global pandemic, was a pivotal moment. This stark contrast between personal joy and global crisis led John to contemplate the world his grandson would inherit. "Panda Demick" emerged as a tool for caretakers to explain the pandemic within the context of the greater environmental crisis facing our planet. The story, featuring a panda named Demick who can communicate with children, animals, and even viruses, aims to provide children with insights into these complex issues in an uplifting and life-affirming manner.

The narrative of "Panda Demick" emphasizes the importance of empathy and helping others. During the pandemic, the dramatic slowing of daily life allowed people to reconnect with family and friends. This theme is depicted through illustrations of family gatherings and the calming of the animal kingdom as the world became quieter. Demick's adventures offer readers a vision of a world in better balance with nature.

John's collaboration with illustrator Jenny Zandona, whom he regards as a daughter, was crucial in bringing "Panda Demick" to life. Jenny's illustrations capture the environmental imbalance preceding the Coronavirus and the transformation of Demick from a worrisome panda to a confident and joyful one. This transformation is skillfully illustrated through a subtle color palette change, culminating in Demick bursting into glorious color, symbolizing his deep love for friends and nature.

The book's emphasis on empathy and helping others resonates with both children and adults, especially during challenging times like a pandemic. One poignant illustration shows a nurse helping a masked elderly patient in a wheelchair, with an empty pair of nurse shoes nearby, representing the front-line healthcare workers lost to the pandemic. This image encapsulates the best and worst of the pandemic experience, facilitating conversations between adults and children about empathy and loss.

John's background in Earth science and high-tech entrepreneurship significantly influenced the themes explored in "Panda Demick." He wanted the story to be more than just about the Coronavirus, offering insight into how a tiny part of nature emerged and reflected an ongoing environmental crisis. His early career at The Greenhouse Gas Project at Scripps Institution of Oceanography, where he met his wife Joan, provided him with a front-row seat to the hard-fact science behind climate change and its impact on ecosystems worldwide for over 45 years.

Panda Demick is not just a children's book; it is a heartfelt message from a grandfather to his grandson and a call to action for future generations to understand and address the environmental challenges we face. Through the story of Demick, John Shay hopes to inspire empathy, understanding, and a deeper connection with nature in readers of all ages.

> "One of my favorite illustrations in the book shows a nurse helping a masked elderly patient in a wheel chair. Resting on the floor next to them is an empty pair of nurse shoes. Those empty shoes represent the front-line healthcare workers we lost to the pandemic. That single image illustrates the best and worst of what we experienced during the pandemic. Children see the empathy of the nurse helping an elderly patient while an adult may recall the suffered losses and be able to offer insight to a child."

John Shay

Literature

Advice for Aspiring Authors

RAVEN HOWELL

> *Writing full time for children the past 3 decades has never gotten old. I still experience the whimsy and wonderment of my youth through words. Being a creative person from childhood- writing, playing an instrument, or drawing, was simply what happened, how I naturally embodied my days.*

by J. Evans

Raven Howell has crafted an impressive career in children's literature, authoring over twenty picture books and contributing to esteemed children's magazines such as Highlights, Cricket, Humpty Dumpty, and The School Magazine. Over her three-decade-long career, she has garnered numerous accolades, including the Excellence in Children's Literature Award, Creative Child Magazine's Best Children's Book Award, Mom's Choice Award, and the NYC Big Book Award. Raven's contributions extend beyond her own books; she writes the Book Bug column for Story Monsters Ink magazine, manages the Kids Corner site, and serves as Publishing Advisor and Creative Director for Red Clover Reader. She also writes for Voice magazine and Reading Gate Publishing, and is a Contributing Author for Reading is Fundamental SoCal and I Am a Promise Books.

Raven's journey into children's literature began in her youth, where creativity was an intrinsic part of her life. She describes a childhood filled with writing, playing musical instruments, and drawing, activities that naturally led her to express herself through words. This innate creativity has been a constant throughout her life, and although her motivation has evolved, the core of her inspiration remains the same. Today, her focus is on inspiring children to read, to love themselves, and to appreciate the world around them and their interactions with others.

Her diverse background, including experiences in the music industry and writing for greeting cards, has significantly influenced her writing style. Raven notes that writing a song is akin to writing a children's poem, as both require rhythm, rhyme, and a beat to be engaging. Similarly, her experience with greeting cards taught her to be concise and to connect with readers on an emotional level. These skills have translated well into her children's poetry and stories, making her work both accessible and impactful.

Nature is a profound source of inspiration for Raven. She finds beauty and magic in the natural world, from rainbows and snowfall to the instinctive behaviors of animals and the intricate details of flowers. Her book "A Star Full of Sky," written entirely under the night sky, exemplifies her deep connection to nature and its influence on her work. Raven's ability to view nature from enchanting angles and translate that wonder into words is a hallmark of her writing.

The influence of her father, a published poet, is another significant aspect of Raven's writing journey. Watching him write for long stretches, jot down ideas, and participate in book events provided her with a model of dedication and passion for the craft. His resonant voice during poetry performances taught her the power of spoken word and its impact on an audience, skills she utilizes during Story Time sessions with children. These experiences have deeply shaped her style and approach to writing.

Raven's books often explore themes of self-esteem, fitting in, and making friends, as seen in titles like "A Colorful Beginning" and "Friends Come in All Sizes." She stays attuned to the evolving needs and interests of young readers through her interactions with the children's community during author visits, book events, and library story times. This engagement ensures that her themes resonate with contemporary young audiences. She gauges the success of her books through sales and positive reviews, indicating that her messages are well-received.

For aspiring children's authors and poets, Raven offers invaluable advice. She emphasizes the importance of developing a unique style and writing in one's own voice, regardless of the platform. Understanding the interests of the target age group and practicing consistently are crucial for improvement. She encourages perseverance, advising aspiring writers to continue pursuing their passion even if immediate success is elusive. Raven's message is clear: dedication and love for the craft will eventually lead to success.

Raven Howell's dedication to children's literature and poetry is evident in her extensive body of work and her efforts to inspire and engage young readers. Her new titles, "Keep Trucking" and "Blink and Glow," continue to bring joy and wonder to children, solidifying her place as a beloved author in the world of children's literature. Through her creative endeavors and commitment to fostering a love for reading, Raven Howell continues to make a lasting impact on young minds.

Business

Why Financial Planning Is a Great Career Option for Women

Financial planning is an increasingly popular and lucrative career for women, offering high salaries, work-life balance, personal fulfillment, and strong support networks, including initiatives, scholarships, and mentorships from the CFP Board.

Financial planning was once thought of as a male-dominated industry, but that's quickly changing. The number of women getting their CERTIFIED FINANCIAL PLANNER™ certification is growing year over year — and for good reason: The benefits of entering this field as a woman are numerous. Below are a few to consider.

• It's lucrative. Financial planners are in high demand and are well-compensated for their expertise. A financial advisor can pull in a generous salary right out of the gate, and earning the right credentials can boost compensation significantly. The median income for those with CFP® certification and less than 5 years of experience is $100,000 — and that median figure grows to $206,000 with 10 or more years of experience. In general, financial advisors with CFP® certification earn 12% more than those without.

• Being a CFP® professional offers good work-life balance. With the potential to work remotely and create one's own schedule, financial planning is a career path well-suited to those looking for flexibility and a desirable work-life balance.

• Financial planning can be personally fulfilling. Providing competent, ethical financial advice that helps others achieve their life goals — from sending their children to college to securing a comfortable retirement — can be extremely gratifying.

Research also finds that female CFP® professionals have a unique dedication to providing holistic financial planning. Working as a financial planner provides opportunities to uplift and empower other women, as well as members of groups historically given fewer opportunities to accumulate wealth.

• Women who aspire to become CFP® professionals will find support in many places. CFP Board, for example, has implemented initiatives to recruit women and advance their careers.

Some firms subsidize the cost of CFP® certification and give employees time away from work to study for the CFP® exam. Additionally, women's networks and business councils can help build leadership skills and professional confidence, and many firms are even paying their employees' membership fees.

CFP Board also administers scholarships for individuals underrepresented in the field, along with a mentoring program.

To learn more and get started today on your path to becoming a CFP® professional, visit getCFPcertified.org.

With demand for personal financial advisors expected to grow significantly in the coming years, and the industry making way for more women professionals, it's worth exploring this rewarding career path.

PHOTO SOURCE: monkeybusinessimages / iStock via Getty Images Plus (StatePoint)

Business

From Courtroom Advocate to Career Coach
The Inspiring Journey of Cordell Parvin

Cordell Parvin transitioned from a successful construction lawyer to a renowned legal coach, inspiring over a thousand lawyers with his practical, storytelling approach to career development and emphasis on personal fulfillment.

Cordell Parvin, a trailblazing legal coach, shares his journey from practicing law to inspiring the next generation of lawyers.

In the high-pressure and demanding realm of law, transitioning from a courtroom advocate to a career coach might appear to be an unusual path. However, for Cordell Parvin, this change has not only reshaped his own career but also inspired and guided over a thousand lawyers throughout the United States and Canada. Parvin's journey from practicing construction law to becoming a celebrated legal coach highlights the significant role of mentorship and personal satisfaction in achieving professional success.

A Legal Career Built on Excellence

Cordell Parvin has become a prominent figure in career development within the legal field, particularly in client acquisition and professional growth for attorneys. With an impressive 38-year career in construction law, Parvin has represented some of the nation's leading contractors. Yet, it was his experience coaching new partners within his law firm that sparked a deeper passion.

In 2004, despite experiencing his most successful professional year, Parvin found greater satisfaction in assisting young lawyers with their career paths. This realization prompted him to leave his practice and fully commit to coaching lawyers. His transition from a high-earning attorney to a full-time coach marks a significant career shift motivated by a desire to make a more meaningful impact on the legal profession.

Practical Coaching Strategies

Parvin's coaching approach is both practical and holistic, concentrating on goal setting, time management, and balancing professional duties with personal life. His strategies are informed by his extensive experience and his roles as a speaker, writer, and blogger on career and client development. Through his engaging presentations at law firms and bar associations, Parvin has established himself as a thought leader in the legal industry.

Since beginning his coaching career in 2005, Parvin has worked with lawyers from various backgrounds, offering invaluable insights into the challenges they encounter. He advocates for a structured approach to professional growth, emphasizing the importance of investing time in both career development and personal well-being. This dual focus is crucial for achieving long-term success and fulfillment in the legal profession.

Engaging Young Lawyers Through Storytelling

Parvin's books, such as "Say Ciao to Chow Mein: Conquering Career Burnout" and "Rising Star," employ a storytelling approach inspired by Ken Blanchard's business parables. These narratives provide serious career advice in a relatable and engaging way, addressing issues like career burnout and the need for a balanced life. By sharing personal anecdotes and practical solutions, Parvin offers young lawyers a roadmap for navigating the complexities of their careers while maintaining their well-being.

Fostering a Collaborative Culture

One of the main challenges in the legal profession is shifting from a competitive mindset to a collaborative one. Parvin stresses the importance of fostering a collaborative culture within law firms, which can be achieved by hiring lawyers with strong interpersonal skills, rewarding teamwork, and prioritizing the development of junior lawyers. This approach not only enhances team dynamics but also creates a more supportive and productive work environment.

Essential Advice for Aspiring Rainmakers

For young lawyers aiming to become successful rainmakers, Parvin's most vital piece of advice is to identify a compelling "why" behind their ambitions. This motivational cornerstone drives the creation of comprehensive plans, which span various timeframes and instill the commitment and discipline required to follow through. By maintaining a clear focus on their goals and understanding their underlying motivations, young lawyers can navigate their careers with greater purpose and determination.

Cordell Parvin's shift from practicing law to coaching has profoundly impacted the careers of countless lawyers. His practical, storytelling approach to career development, combined with his emphasis on personal fulfillment and collaborative culture, provides invaluable guidance to young lawyers. Parvin's journey serves as an inspiring testament to the power of mentorship and the importance of pursuing a career that aligns with one's passions and values.

Cordell Parvin is a visionary mentor whose transformative coaching empowers lawyers to achieve professional success and personal fulfillment.

PHOTO: *Enis Hulli, General Partner at 500 Emerging Europe, is redefining the future of innovation in the regional startup ecosystem.*

Pioneering Global Success from Emerging Europe
ENIS HULLI
Bridging the Gap Between Regional Talent and Global Markets

BY ONAT ONCU

Enis Hulli, General Partner at 500 Emerging Europe, discusses his journey, investment philosophy, and strategies for transforming regional startups into global competitors by bridging Emerging Europe with Silicon Valley.

In the dynamic world of entrepreneurship, few figures have made as significant an impact as Enis Hulli, General Partner at 500 Emerging Europe. With a solid foundation in engineering and a deep understanding of the startup ecosystem, Enis has been instrumental in unlocking the global potential of regional startups. His journey from establishing firstseed, an early-stage investment network, to becoming a key player at 500 Emerging Europe highlights his unwavering dedication to fostering innovation and growth. Enis's mission goes beyond mere investment; he is committed to transforming Emerging Europe into a hub of global entrepreneurial success.

Enis Hulli's achievements in the venture capital arena are truly commendable. His strategic insights and commitment to excellence have elevated 500 Emerging Europe to a prominent position within the global startup community. By creating a vital link between Emerging Europe and Silicon Valley, Enis has empowered numerous entrepreneurs to expand their reach and realize their global ambitions. His efforts have not only driven the success of individual startups but have also redefined the venture capital landscape in the region. As you explore this engaging interview, you'll gain a deeper understanding of the vision and expertise that make Enis Hulli a pioneering force in entrepreneurship.

Can you share a bit about your career journey and what led you to become a General Partner at 500 Emerging Europe?

Bored during my college years, I found myself wondering about different business ideas and eventually co-founded a start-up while I was only 20. Looking back, I definitely was not cut out for it and the company eventually failed. I tried my luck joining Rocket Internet for a brief timeframe but they soon decided to shut down that venture entirely. This experience pushed me in a more risk-averse direction, as I started to make money installing HVAC systems for a few years – leveraging my Civil Engineering degree only to feel unfulfilled and hungry to be able to spend my time at a job where I can learn and grow more.

This is the core reason why I delved into books and podcasts about entrepreneurship and started angel investing after I made some money. It eventually turned into an angel network and around the same time I met with 500 Startups. The opportunity to be able to take

Business

a stab at building my own venture capital fund was just too good to refuse so I slowly winded down the HVAC operations and jumped ship to build my own fund as a 25-year old.

What were some of the biggest challenges you faced when you first entered the venture capital industry, and how did you overcome them?

As a 25-year-old with no substantial track record and a failed start-up experience, it was challenging to gain people's trust. It took me two years to gather a few supporters to help build an angel network. Angel networks are different from VC funds since their investors do have a say in how the money is allocated. For a young person with a contrarian thesis and strong self-belief, the most significant hurdle is earning enough trust initially to build upon. The initial believers are crucial as they pave the way to success. Building trust, demonstrating strong commitment, and showing momentum are critical to gaining enough support to overcome that first major hurdle.

Enis Hulli is a visionary leader, transforming Emerging Europe's startup ecosystem with strategic insight and unwavering dedication to innovation.

Can you elaborate on your investment philosophy and the criteria you look for when evaluating potential start-ups?

Emerging Europe is distinct from other emerging markets, or even European funds, in that all unicorns are globally oriented companies. The successful companies in Emerging Europe generate revenues from international markets, raise capital from international VCs, and plan for exits or IPOs in international markets. The thesis revolves around betting on local talent potential while hedging against other market factors, from early customers to scaling revenue to fundraising. This necessitates a different investment thesis than a typical VC, who is making a significant bet within their geography across multiple dimensions.

Our thesis on finding global success stories from Emerging Europe turns traditional scouting on its head. Instead of simply seeking the best entrepreneurs in the region, we look for the best entrepreneurs globally who are from Emerging Europe and are inclined to build their technology teams here. The number of opportunities is much more limited when you aim for all your companies to compete globally, but the potential scale of these opportunities is much higher. Given this finite nature of opportunities, our thesis revolves around maximizing access to the best deals.

What are some unique opportunities and challenges you see in the start-up ecosystem of Emerging Europe?

To hedge against the liquidity crunch in the region, we aim to find entrepreneurs with a global focus who can secure their next round of financing from international investors. This creates a financing value chain drift, where a start-up initially engaging with VCs from Emerging Europe can eventually attract Silicon Valley investors. Historical success stories from the region validate this thesis, as all unicorns have raised the majority of their funding from US investors. Similarly, our portfolio has raised over $1 billion, predominantly from the US.

This presents a significant challenge for founders, who sometimes have to relocate prematurely at the pre-seed stage to build a network in the Bay Area. Starting with the right early customers and design partners, they quickly move into fundraising mode, aiming to onboard US VCs. While this strategy has obvious long-term benefits, it also involves compromises in the short term concerning team culture, product development speed, and foregoing easily attainable customers in the region.

The biggest opportunity lies in the exceptional talent available in Emerging Europe. We anchor ourselves to this belief and invest in founders who are looking to capitalize on that.

How do you see 500 Emerging Europe contributing to the broader start-up ecosystem in the region?

We position ourselves as a bridge between Emerging Europe and Silicon Valley. This is crucial because start-ups in Emerging Europe strive to emulate Silicon Valley despite being away. The increase in the number of funds with a similar thesis to ours following our success is crucial for the region. 70% of all founders we backed are in Silicon Valley, having moved either before or shortly after our investment.

Strengthening this bridge can first create multiple ecosystems in Emerging Europe that resemble those of Israel, and eventually even position Emerging Europe as a true competitor to Silicon Valley. This approach leverages the region's advantages while fully hedging against its disadvantages.

What advice would you give to entrepreneurs who are looking to secure funding and grow their start-ups?

Founders often make many unconscious decisions, especially at the beginning, and choosing which region to focus on is one of these. Concentrating on customers from your first or second-degree connections might position you as a regional start-up, which would later limit your fundraising options.

Fundraising is a proximity game, especially at the early stages, and a local or regional positioning would drastically reduce the pool of potential investors. We back founders who aim to position themselves and their start-ups on a global scale, opening the door to attracting international funds. This strategy increases their flexibility to fundraise and maximizes their upside potential.

Source: This content is inspired by an interview originally published in Entrepreneur Prime magazine.

Business

Pioneering Strategic HR Leadership

CANDICE ELLIOTT

Candice Elliott, Fractional CHRO in Santa Cruz, CA, shares her expertise in strategic HR leadership and innovation.

The Hearth Podcast's new season explores HR's evolving role as a strategic thought partner, featuring expert insights on integrating HR into business strategy and fostering innovation for organizational success.

In an exciting development for human resources professionals and enthusiasts, The Hearth Podcast has announced the launch of its new season, focusing on the evolving role of HR as a thought partner within organizations. This season promises to delve into the transformative impact HR can have when integrated as a strategic partner in business operations.

The Hearth Podcast, known for its insightful discussions and expert interviews, aims to shed light on the dynamic nature of HR in today's rapidly changing business environment. As companies increasingly recognize the value of human capital, HR's role is shifting from traditional administrative functions to becoming a pivotal player in strategic decision-making processes.

This season will feature a series of episodes that explore various aspects of HR's evolving role. Listeners can expect to hear from industry leaders, HR experts, and thought leaders who will share their experiences and insights on how HR can drive organizational success. Topics will include the integration of HR in strategic planning, the importance of fostering a culture of innovation, and the ways in which HR can contribute to achieving business objectives.

The podcast aims to provide valuable perspectives on how HR professionals can position themselves as thought partners, capable of influencing and guiding organizational strategy. By highlighting real-world examples and best practices, The Hearth Podcast seeks to inspire HR professionals to embrace their roles as strategic partners and thought leaders.

Listeners can tune in to the new season of The Hearth Podcast on major streaming platforms. Whether you are an HR professional looking to enhance your strategic impact or a business leader seeking to understand the value of HR as a thought partner, this season promises to offer valuable insights and practical advice.

As the business landscape continues to evolve, The Hearth Podcast remains committed to exploring the critical role of HR in shaping the future of work. Don't miss out on this opportunity to gain a deeper understanding of how HR can drive innovation and success in your organization.

KEY TAKEAWAYS FROM THE EPISODE:

- Embracing practices like locally sourcing food and biodynamic agriculture can inspire the creation of healthier and more resilient work environments.

- Prioritizing sustainable practices can counteract the negative impacts of industrialization, benefiting both people and the environment.

- Cultivating grounding and connection in hybrid and remote work settings enhances employee well-being and fosters a supportive culture.

- Effective workload management promotes sustained productivity while ensuring employees remain balanced and energized.

- Developing a strong social infrastructure within organizations supports employees in caring for children and elders, fostering a deeper sense of connection and community.

Business

Carver Bancorp, Inc. Appoints Donald Felix as New President and CEO

Carver Bancorp, Inc. appoints Donald Felix as President and CEO, effective November 1, 2024, to drive growth and innovation, reinforcing its commitment to community development and financial inclusion.

PHOTO: Felix brings more than two decades of banking leadership to advance Carver into its next era of growth.
Photo courtesy of Carver Bank.

In a significant leadership transition, Carver Bancorp, Inc. has announced the appointment of Donald Felix as its new President and Chief Executive Officer, effective November 1, 2024. This strategic move marks a new chapter for the renowned financial institution, which has been a cornerstone in community banking.

Donald Felix brings a wealth of experience and a visionary approach to his new role at Carver Bancorp. With a distinguished career in the banking sector, Felix is poised to lead the company into a new era of growth and innovation. His appointment is expected to bolster Carver's commitment to serving its community and expanding its reach in the financial industry.

Felix succeeds the outgoing CEO, who has been instrumental in steering the company through challenging times and setting a solid foundation for future success. Under Felix's leadership, Carver Bancorp aims to enhance its service offerings and strengthen its position as a leader in community banking.

The board of directors expressed their confidence in Felix's ability to drive the company forward, citing his impressive track record and dedication to fostering inclusive financial solutions. As Carver Bancorp looks to the future, stakeholders and customers alike are eager to see the positive impact of Felix's leadership.

Stay tuned as Carver Bancorp embarks on this exciting new journey under the guidance of Donald Felix, promising a future filled with innovation, growth, and community-focused initiatives.

DONALD FELIX

Prior to his employment with Carver, Mr. Felix served as Executive Vice President of Citizens Financial Group, Head of National Banking & Expansion from 2021 to 2023. Before that, he served as Managing Director of JPMorgan Chase, in the Consumer Bank as Head of Consumer Financial Health from 2019 to 2021. He was also the Chief of Staff in the Office of the CEO, for Chase Consumer Bank & Wealth Management, from 2016 to 2019, and before joining Chase held various senior positions domestically and abroad at Citi from 1996 to 2016.

He holds an MBA in Finance and Strategic Management from The Wharton School, University of Pennsylvania, and a BBA in Information Systems and Analysis from Howard University. He is a Director at the Urban League of Eastern Massachusetts.

A first-generation Caribbean-American, Mr. Felix was born and raised in New York City and has a deep connection and long history of civic engagement with the communities that Carver serves.

- Carver is a historic institution founded in 1948 to help underserved communities in New York City build wealth.

- Carver continues to pay its mission forward, focusing on Minority and Women Business Enterprises and the growing middle-income neighborhoods it serves.

- Approximately $0.80 of each deposit dollar at the Bank is reinvested in the diverse communities it serves through competitively priced loan capital.

- Donald Felix is only the sixth CEO in Carver's 76-year history.

Business

Frederik Steensgaard discusses BeCause's innovative approach to sustainability in hospitality, emphasizing AI's role, overcoming industry challenges, and aligning with global climate commitments for a greener future.

Frederik Steensgaard, CEO of BeCause, leading the charge in sustainable hospitality innovation with a commitment to environmental responsibility.

Leading the Charge

FREDERIK STEENSGAARD

HOW BeCause IS TRANSFORMING THE HOTEL INDUSTRY WITH AI-POWERED SUSTAINABILITY SOLUTIONS

BY ONAT ONCU

Frederik Steensgaard is a visionary leader at the forefront of sustainable innovation in the hospitality industry. As the CEO and Co-Founder of BeCause, he has transformed the way hotels manage their sustainability data, making it easier and more cost-effective for them to meet their environmental goals. Under his leadership, BeCause has become a pivotal player in the industry, helping over 22,000 companies, including major hotel groups like Radisson and platforms like Booking.com, to streamline their sustainability efforts. Frederik's commitment to sustainability extends beyond his company; he is an active member of the Climate Committee at the Danish Industry Federation, where he contributes to shaping policies that promote environmental responsibility. His academic background in business, sociology, and entrepreneurship from the Copenhagen Business School further underscores his dedication to creating impactful solutions that benefit both businesses and the planet.

In this exclusive interview with Entrepreneur Prime Magazine, Frederik shares insights into the journey of founding BeCause, the challenges faced, and the innovative solutions that have propelled the company to success. He discusses the critical role of AI in preventing greenwashing and enhancing sustainability

Business

reporting, as well as BeCause's alignment with the objectives of the Paris Agreement. Frederik also offers valuable advice for aspiring entrepreneurs looking to make a difference in the realm of sustainability. His passion for travel and the environment, combined with his expertise in technology and management, make Frederik Steensgaard a true pioneer in driving the hospitality industry towards a greener future.

What motivated you and Jonas Jacobsen to found BeCause?

Jonas and I met while working on a project for a global healthcare technology company, and we immediately connected over our shared frustration with the slow advancement of sustainability-focused initiatives in the market. People expressed a desire to be more sustainable in their everyday lives everywhere we looked, but in many cases, the market failed to supply transparent and trustworthy solutions.

With Jonas' engineering background and my experience in management consulting, we believed that by connecting sustainability ecosystems with the right technology infrastructure, we could

> Frederik Steensgaard is a trailblazer in sustainable innovation, transforming hospitality with visionary leadership and groundbreaking technology solutions.

drive (and accelerate) industries toward a greener future.

We decided to start with the travel sector, specifically hospitality, for several reasons. First, we knew there was a strong demand for more sustainable hotel options, but there were few ways for consumers to find and book those choices. Travel also holds a personal significance for me. Growing up in Oman, I witnessed the degradation of coral reefs due to various factors, including tourism, which impacted me. Finding ways to reduce travel's impact on local environments became a passion of mine.

Can you describe the main challenges you faced when launching BeCause in 2021 and how you overcame them?

When we launched BeCause, we asked hotels and booking platforms to completely change how they managed sustainability data, as their processes were fragmented, siloed and manual.

As with any startup, we had to prove how moving to our model—a centralized, shared platform that can synergize and automatically communicate hotel sustainability data across stakeholders, from hotels and booking platforms to green certification entities and regulators—could help them drive new business, increase access to sustainability data, and significantly reduce their operational costs.

Honestly, it took a while to get this innovation off the ground initially. We needed to develop a complex product suite accommodating multiple types of market stakeholders and then educate and convince the market of this model.

Thankfully, we found wonderful partners in Booking.com, Radisson Hotel Group, and Green Key. They quickly understood our vision and recognized the uniqueness and value of our solution from each of their company perspectives. Their support has been instrumental in our exponential growth since then.

Another challenge we faced early on was the general industry awareness about the growing tidal wave of sustainability demands that were about to hit businesses in travel, tourism and hospitality. However, this has subsided, with the various new regulatory frameworks and industry-wide standards making the issue and priority clear and urgent across the entire industry.

How does BeCause facilitate connecting hotels and sustainability solution providers to address specific issues?

By assembling all stakeholders of the travel ecosystem and their data in a central hub, we empower decision-makers with the data analysis and options they need to improve their sustainability data and the performance of their businesses. Whether it's the measurement of their carbon emissions, reduction of their food waste, or providing strategic consulting BeCause helps companies identify their sustainability challenges and match hotels with data and solution providers specialized in their individual needs. Our model creates a triple win: benefiting the hotel in need, the vendor providing the solution, and promoting planetary sustainability.

How do you envision the role of AI evolving in BeCause's platform to prevent issues like greenwashing and enhance sustainability reporting?

We already use AI today to facilitate data reuse, enabling hotels to collect a metric once and then have our platform automatically map it to meet various stakeholder requirements. For example, a sustainability metric collected for the European Sustainability Reporting Standards (ESRS), which helps hotels meet their obligations under the EU's Corporate Sustainability Reporting Directive (CSRD), can also be used to comply with voluntary certifications like Green Key, RFPs requested by corporate travelers, and industry standards, e.g., Hotel Sustainability Basics, with little manual effort.

The AI layer in BeCause also increasingly identifies information gaps and potential input errors, automates workflows, and recommends actions. For example, if a hotel is a few metrics away from qualifying for Green Key certification, the platform can nudge the property to collect this missing information. This creates an ecosystem where it's far more accessible and less expensive to obtain certification, which is the best way for hotels to prove their commitment to sustainability and minimize greenwashing.

How does BeCause align its sustainability goals and initiatives with the objectives of the Paris Agreement, and what role do you see your platform playing in helping the tourism industry meet these international climate commitments?

One can only manage what is measured, and what is measured typically becomes managed. Our primary role is enabling and supporting this virtuous cycle as the world demands it.

Firstly, by helping hotels and tourism operators collect and report sustainability data, they can significantly improve awareness and transparency across their operational footprint and unique impact potential, positive and negative. This gives them the insights and levers needed to make bold moves towards meeting and exceeding their international climate commitments.

I believe CSRD is the jumping-off point for greater sustainability across industries worldwide. While it directly pertains only to the EU, more countries have and will introduce mandatory corporate sustainability reporting to meet their obligations under the Paris Agreement, and private market frameworks similarly align with CSRD as the de facto standard.

BeCause makes compliance with CSRD and many other pertinent frameworks easier in one go. As an industry-specific sustainability data management platform, we've sifted through the thousands of data points in ESRS to pull out the ones relevant to the hotel and tourism industries. Without BeCause, the process of collecting, coordinating, validating and reporting is overly complicated, time-consuming and costly, if at all feasible for the typical budgets and resources of hotels. With BeCause, we can get this done dramatically simpler, faster, and cheaper.

What advice would you give to other entrepreneurs looking to create technology solutions to enhance sustainability in various industries?

While it would be great if companies were motivated by pure altruism when it comes to sustainability, to be successful, your solution needs to clearly illustrate how it benefits these companies financially or operationally. Aim to solve those pain points in the process rather than using greater sustainability as your sole objective (even if it is unmistakably critical). In other words, when it comes to enhancing sustainability, the keyword is a classic but true buzzword--create synergy. Our intense focus on this has enabled our company to break through and accelerate our growth.

Source: This content is inspired by an interview originally published in Entrepreneur Prime magazine.

Beauty

PHOTO: The heart of Dar Barot's artistry - his salon near Buckingham Palace - where dreams of beauty come true.

The Creative Maestro Redefining Beauty - From Hollywood to Royalty

The man behind towering hair creations, Dar Barot, has been an influential force in the hairstyling industry for over 40 years.

In the world of hairstyling, one name stands out like no other - Dar Barot. Famously dubbed as 'Mr Big' by Tatler, Dar has been the genius behind towering hair creations in fashion shoots and videos for over four decades. From A-list celebrities to international royalty, his skills have graced the tresses of the most distinguished personalities, leaving an indelible mark on the beauty industry. Beauty Prime had the honor of sitting down with the maestro himself to unravel the journey that made him an icon and the secrets behind his success.

A Journey of Passion and Creativity

Dar Barot's illustrious career commenced in 1973 when he joined the legendary Vidal Sassoon salon in London. Learning from the maestro himself, Dar honed cutting techniques that focused on sculpting hair to enhance facial beauty and bone structure. His career took flight in the 1980s when he embarked on a freelance journey, working with esteemed photographers like Norman Parkinson, David Bailey, and Lord Patrick Lichfield. His impeccable skills and creative vision caught the eye of the fashion world, leading him to style pop icons like Paul McCartney, Boy George, and Kate Bush.

In 1983, Dar took a bold step forward, opening his first salon, Dar Salon, in London. This endeavor was supported by his business partner, Imran Khan. Throughout the 1980s and 90s, his reputation soared as he worked on fashion shoots and established himself as a force to be reckoned with in the hairstyling industry.

The Power of 'Total Look'

Beauty

The Master of Hairdressing Unveils His Secrets to Timeless Beauty

One of Dar Barot's greatest strengths lies in his ability to craft a 'total look' for his clients. Beyond hair, he excels in fashion styling and makeup, designing a bespoke hairstyle that complements the individual's lifestyle, facial features, and bone structure. His precision-cutting skills, acquired from top-tier salons, create 'wash-n-go' styles that are effortlessly maintained at home. With his Indian heritage, Dar seamlessly unites Western and Eastern styling, bringing a unique perspective to the world of beauty.

As a former editor for Asian Fashion Magazine, equivalent to Marie Claire, Dar's expertise and understanding of beauty go beyond borders, catering to diverse clientele with finesse.

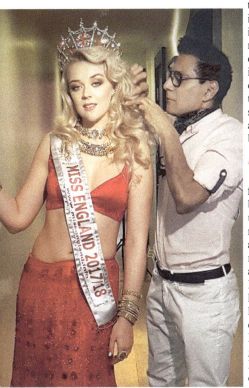

PHOTO: Miss England 2017-2018 Stephani Hill and Dar Barrot

Clientele of Celebrities and Royalty

When you boast a clientele that includes Hollywood stars and international royalty, there's no denying your prowess. Among his impressive list of clients, Dar has worked with icons like Goldie Hawn, Britt Ekland, Aishwarya Rai, and Katie Derham. His artistry has also graced the tresses of esteemed figures like the Sultana of Pahang, the Queen of Malaysia, and His Royal Highness Prince Sufi of Brunei.

Setting the Trends

In the ever-evolving world of hairstyling, Dar Barot stands tall as a trendsetter rather than a follower. He confidently claims to set the trends himself, from sleek bobs to tumbling curls and age-defying longer cuts. His revolutionary volumizing 'Dar Cut' has garnered admiration and popularity, giving clients the illusion of thicker hair.

In recent times, Dar's creative ingenuity unleashed London's fashionable blunt bob cut, featured on the front cover of the Daily Mail, proving that he continues to push boundaries and captivate the beauty industry.

Words of Wisdom for Aspiring Hairstylists

For those aspiring to make their mark in the hairstyling industry, Dar Barot has a piece of invaluable advice: "Never go into hairdressing to become rich. This industry is all about creativity." Emphasizing the importance of a keen eye and creative ability, he believes true mastery lies in understanding each facial feature and enhancing a woman's beauty.

A Vision for Scalp Nourishment

As a visionary with a passion for excellence, Dar Barot looks beyond mainstream beauty products. While he has worked with renowned companies like Wella and L'Oreal, he feels that nothing matches the traditional Indian approach to nourishing the scalp. His upcoming venture involves launching a range of Ayurvedic hair oils, drawing inspiration from centuries-old techniques used by Indian women. Recognizing that good hair starts from the scalp, Dar seeks to revolutionize hair care with this fusion of tradition and modernity.

Dar Barot's journey from Vidal Sassoon to becoming a global hairstyling icon is a testament to his passion, creativity, and dedication to the art of beauty. With his 'total look' approach, trendsetting capabilities, and commitment to scalp nourishment, he continues to redefine the standards of beauty, leaving an everlasting impact on the industry and his clients' lives alike.

Beauty

ELENA'S HAIRCARE ODYSSEY
Empowering Women's Wellness Journey

Elena's salon introduces cutting-edge treatments like Botox for hair and NANOPLASTICA, captivating clients from all over the world.

BOURNEMOUTH- Meet Elena, the 31-year-old trailblazer who revolutionized haircare in the South of England with her straightening salon and an array of exceptional treatments. In an exclusive interview with Beauty Prime, Elena shares her inspiring journey from an air traffic controller to a renowned hair expert, offering valuable insights and advice for aspiring professionals.*

From the Skies to Stunning Strands

Elena's career path may seem like a captivating plot twist, as she never envisioned herself becoming a hair expert. With an academic background in the Aviation Academy and several years of experience as an air traffic controller in Belarus, her life took an unexpected turn when she moved to Bournemouth in 2018.

As Elena's curls and frizz have been a constant challenge, she decided to try a hair treatment for the first time - the life-changing moment that altered her destiny forever. The remarkable results of the treatment ignited a passion in her to share the magic with others. Driven by the desire to transform hair into a manageable, soft, and frizz-free state, she set forth on an extraordinary journey to create her dream job.

Passion, Dedication, and Client Care

One of the keys to Elena's success is her unwavering dedication and passion for her craft. Her love for hair treatments, such as KERATIN BOTOX and NANOPLASTICA, shines through in her work, and clients can't help but notice the difference. With a specialized focus on straightening and conditioning treatments, Elena's salon has gained recognition and loyalty from numerous satisfied clients, many of whom keep coming back for more.

But it doesn't stop there; Elena's enthusiasm extends beyond her salon's walls. As a teacher, she motivates and inspires her students, imparting her knowledge and success stories to aspiring professionals from not just across the UK but also from various parts of Europe and the world. Her online courses have attracted over 200 students, proving that her passion knows no geographical boundaries.

Unveiling the Secret to Success

Elena's salon has become synonymous with groundbreaking hair treatments. By focusing on advanced straightening and conditioning techniques, she stays ahead of the curve. Elena has been a pioneer in introducing innovative treatments like Botox for hair and NANOPLASTICA in the UK, making her salon a sought-after destination for haircare enthusiasts.

Her secret to success lies in customizing treatments based on individual hair types and desired results. With a range of over 15 different products, Elena ensures that even the most challenging hair types find solace in her salon's services. The allure of long-lasting straightening and conditioning without the hassle of daily styling has sparked the interest of clients from far and wide, some traveling several hours to experience the magic firsthand.

A Dreamer with a Vision

Elena's journey is a testament to the power of dreaming big and believing in oneself. From humble beginnings in a small room with second-hand furniture to owning a luxurious salon on Main Street, her determination and passion have shattered barriers. Despite challenges, including managing a salon while caring for her baby, Elena's unwavering love for her craft has proven that one can achieve greatness with perseverance.

Her dreams don't stop at her salon's success. Elena aspires to travel the world, teaching her exceptional treatments to aspiring professionals everywhere. With a vision of opening more salons across the UK and even reaching far-off lands like America and Australia, her entrepreneurial spirit knows no bounds.

Elena's journey from air traffic controller to haircare visionary is nothing short of inspiring. Her dedication, passion, and devotion to her craft have transformed her salon into a haven for those seeking remarkable straightening and conditioning treatments. Elena's story reminds us that with determination, belief in oneself, and an unyielding passion for what you do, achieving greatness is possible. So, to all the dreamers out there, never stop dreaming, for you too can turn your dreams into reality, just like Elena.

PHOTO: From humble beginnings to owning a luxurious salon, Elena's story is a testament to the power of dreams and determination.

Get dolled up right Seduire London

Pamela Kennedy is a Skincare Specialist and Owner of Seduire London Beauty Clinic, located in the heart of London's Soho Square. Pamela Kennedy trained in the industry 11 years ago when she had her second son in 2014. Then she decided to start her own beauty clinic to help give her some flexibility. Her passion has always been skincare. She loves researching and finding new treatments and products to keep the skin youthful without being too intrusive. When they first started she always wanted to find alternatives to enhance clients natural beauty and not completely change it. We have featured in the sun newspaper, closer and OK magazine plus the evening standard.

"My Favorite beauty treatment would have to be caci the on surgical facelift, it is basically gym for the face using microcurrent to strengthen muscles and sagging skin I love the results when we perform these treatments, It also does treatments for the body such as our bum lift treatment which is very

"My Favorite beauty treatment would have to be caci the on surgical facelift, it is basically gym for the face using microcurrent to strengthen muscles and sagging skin I love the results when we perform these treatments"

popular." said in response to our question what is your favorite beauty treadment?. She continued that "You can see results from your very first treatment but the more you have the better it gets. Most of our high end clients such as michelle collins , we recently gave her caci facials before her wedding day and laura whitmore they love caci facials. We have also treated stars such as Bruno Tonioli and Gabby Roslin."

She said that "If I was to give any advice for those coming into this industry it would be to train train train, the industry is so quick moving and technology and research is constantly upgrading you can never know it all you have to keep learning, I stay up to date by always researching new treatments and learning new techniques to help improve my knowledge."

Having three children and a business Pamela finds her beauty routine has to be quick and effective prevention is better than cure where skin is concerned so she uses the jan marini 5 step skincare Management system. "It's simple and effective. I can take some steps out and only use three when I'm in a rush and my skin feels incredible after I use it." she says. Pamela's one key tip for everyone who asks about their skin is that SPF is always a must for every season, use it every single day, come rain or shine.

Beauty

PHOTO: Simone Thomas, Founder of Simone Thomas Wellness, on a mission to empower women's wellness and restore confidence through holistic approaches.

Empowering Women's Wellness Journey:
SIMONE THOMAS'S INSPIRING STORY

By Dan Peters

Simone Thomas, a successful entrepreneur, mother of two, and passionate advocate for women's health and wellness, has embarked on a journey that not only transformed her own life but also touched the lives of many others. Through her personal struggles with health conditions and hair loss, she discovered the power of nutrition and self-care, which led her to create the multi-award-winning Simone Thomas Wellness range. In this article, we delve into Simone's inspiring story, her approach to running a successful business, and the focus she places on staff happiness and customer engagement.

The Path to Wellness

Simone's wellness journey began in her early twenties when she faced health challenges, including being diagnosed with IBD and endometriosis. The impact of these conditions extended to hair thinning and hair loss, leaving her feeling utterly helpless. As a woman planning for a family, her health and well-being became paramount. This

Beauty

PHOTO: Unlock Your Wellness Potential with Simone Thomas Wellness - Nourishing Your Mind, Body, and Soul with Natural Goodness.

experience ignited her passion for understanding the crucial role of diet and nutrition in gut health, skin condition, and hair health, particularly the significance of supplementation.

Simone's quest to regain her health and confidence became the catalyst for her desire to help others struggling with similar issues. Thus, the birth of the multi-award-winning Simone Thomas Wellness range, designed to empower individuals and restore their confidence and self-esteem at different stages of their lives.

Running the Business with Joy and Passion

Running a successful business that caters to various aspects of wellness is no small feat, but Simone finds joy in her daily pursuits. Even amidst the stress of meeting international deadlines and managing distributors worldwide, Simone's team and the exciting adventures they share bring her daily delight. Her unique approach to her company makes it feel less like work and more like a passion-driven endeavor.

Simone attributes her success to her incredible team, who have been with her for years and run her wellness clinic and hair salon with efficiency. As a busy mom of two, time is precious, and she ensures she looks after herself to maintain the energy needed to keep up with her children.

Engaging Customers and Staff

At Simone's wellness clinic and salon, engaging customers and creating a positive attentive environment are top priorities. Through monthly newsletters, clients receive valuable information and wellness advice, fostering a sense of connection and trust. Moreover, the "refer a friend" scheme has been highly successful, leveraging the power of word-of-mouth marketing from satisfied customers.

Simone also uses creative giveaways, like offering free haircuts and blow-dries to people with specific names, to boost social media engagement and interactions. These initiatives not only generate excitement but also convert many winners into loyal, long-term customers.

Taking Care of Staff and Staying Current

Staff happiness and a pleasant work environment are essential to Simone. The salon boasts great music, candles, and a calm atmosphere to ensure both customers and staff feel relaxed and welcomed. Continuous training is also a cornerstone of the business, keeping the team up-to-date with industry trends and new products, ensuring they remain at the cutting edge of their expertise.

Simone's Daily Routine

Despite her demanding international schedule, Simone makes sure to prioritize "ME time." With a disciplined routine, she manages to juggle her responsibilities as a mother, businesswoman, and advocate for wellness. Early mornings start with a lemon water infusion, followed by a nutritious Simone Thomas Wellness protein smoothie. This sets the tone for a productive day that includes time at the gym, Pilates, or beach walks. Fridays offer a chance for her to unwind and connect with friends and her children in a relaxed setting.

Simone Thomas's inspiring journey from personal struggles to creating a successful wellness empire exemplifies the transformative power of self-care, dedication, and passion. Her commitment to helping others achieve their best selves while fostering a positive work environment for her team and loyal customers is commendable. Through Simone's approach to wellness, many individuals have regained their confidence and embraced a healthier lifestyle, making her an exemplary figure in the field of wellness and entrepreneurship.

PHOTO: Simone and her passionate team of experts at the wellness clinic, dedicated to providing top-notch care and support for their clients.

Available in
PRINT

Americas to Australia Europe to Africa Reader's House is available over 190 countries and thousands of retaiers, platforms including Amazon, Barnes & Noble, Walmart, Waterstone's .....

ELECTRONIC

It is an electronic (flip book) format and interactive. Accessable from electronic devices like pc, smart phone, notepads..

ONLINE

All interviews, we conduct make them accessable online for free.

SOCIAL MEDIA

We are on Facebook, Instagram and X. Please follow us on social media @novelistpost

contact us today for an interview opportunity at
editor@novelistpost.com

Save up to 50% when you order 10 or more from the same issue

YES! I would like a subscription to

- [ ] Current Issue for
- [ ] One-Year Subscription (_____ Issues) for
- [ ] Two-Year Subscription (_____ Issues) for
  - [ ] I am a renewing a current subscription   [ ] I am a new subscriber

Name: _____   Phone: _____

Shipping Address: _____

Billing Address: _____

Email: _____

☐ Yes, I would like to receive updates, newsletters and special offers
☐ No, I would NOT like to receive updates, newsletters and special offers

Payment Type: [ ] Check   [ ] Bank transfer   [ ] Wise   [ ] PayPal

_____
_____

Please mail this form to:
Magazine Name:

Subscribe Now!

Milton Keynes UK
Ingram Content Group UK Ltd.
UKHW051831231024
449918UK00005B/17